A
Concise Companion
and Commentary
for
The New
Catholic Catechism

A
Concise Companion
and Commentary
for
The New
Catholic Catechism

Fr. James Tolhurst

In honore S Roberti Bellarmini, viri doctissimi, corde caritate infusi, auctori exemplaris.

First published in 1994

Gracewing
Fowler Wright Books
Southern Ave, Leominster
Herefordshire HR6 0QF
United Kingdom

Christian Classics
PO Box 30
Westminster
Maryland 21157
USA

Distributed

In New Zealand by
Catholic Supplies Ltd
80 Adelaide Rd
Wellington
New Zealand

In Australia by
Charles Paine Pty
8 Ferris Street
North Parramatta
NSW 2151 Australia

IMPRIMI POTEST
Paul Chavasse STL
Provost Cong Orat

NIHIL OBSTAT
Ieuan Wyn Jones,
Censor

6 October. 1993

IMPRIMATUR
John Aloysius Ward
OFM Cap,
Archbishop of Cardiff
18 October. 1993

The translation of *Fidei Depositum* is the authorised text published in *L'Osservatore Romano*.

The *Nihil Obstat* and *Imprimatur* are a declaration that a book or pamphlet is considered to be free from doctrinal or moral error. It is not implied that those who have granted the *Nihil Obstat* and *Imprimatur* agree with the contents, opinions or statements expressed.

Typesetting by Action Typesetting Limited, Gloucester

Printed in Great Britain by The Cromwell Press.
Broughton Gifford, Melksham, Wiltshire SN12 8PH

UK ISBN 085244 253 X
US ISBN 087061 203 4

CONTENTS

PART TWO: THE CELEBRATION OF THE CHRISTIAN MYSTERY

PART FOUR: CHRISTIAN PRAYER

PREFACE

Catechisms stem from the need to provide an explanation for the faith that we have received and in which we are baptised. We can see the outlines in Philip's encounter with the treasurer of the Queen of Ethiopia in Acts 8,27f and in the summaries of I Cor 11,23 and 15,3f. They developed into the formal instructions given by bishops like S. Cyril of Jerusalem in the fourth century

By the eighth century S. Bede is recommending to Egbert, bishop of York that priests should be made to explain to their parishioners the Creed and the Our Father in the native tongue. It was only a short step to producing question and answer *catechisms* which began to emerge in the ninth century. A structure also developed around the Creed, the Commandments, the Sacraments and the Our Father. The Council of Lambeth in 1281 instructed the clergy to preach four times a year on "the fourteen articles of the Creed, the ten commandments, the precepts of the Gospel ... the seven works of mercy, the seven capital sins, the seven principal virtues, and the seven sacraments of grace without any fantastic weaving or subtle adornment"[1]. Luther based his *kleiner katechismus* in 1529 on just these principles. So also did S. Peter Canisius and S. Robert Bellarmine who replied for the Catholic side.[2]

The most famous however was the *Roman Catechism* known as the Catechism of the Council of Trent, authorised by S. Pius V on 28 September 1566. It was divided into four sections: The Apostles' Creed, the Sacraments, the Ten Commandments and the Lord's Prayer.

By the time of Vatican I, Pius IX was in favour of producing a new uniform catechism and forty one bishops spoke on the subjct between 10 and 22 February, 1870. The matter was referred to a papal commission because there was no agreement about local adaptions and the overall format.[3] This left the responsibility to local hierarchies, who published catechisms of their own. The *Baltimore Catechism* was produced in 1884 and the English and Welsh bishops followed with the *Catechism of Christian Doctine* in 1889. The question of a catechism for the whole Church arose during Vatican II, but again no consensus was achieved and the bishops decided that a directory should be issued[4] which appeared in 1971.

[1.] Mansi: *Sacrorum Concilio, ... collectio,* 1759. XXIV p. 410.
[2.] S. Robert Bellarmine's *Dottrina Cristiana breve* of 1597 ran to 62 language editions.
[3.] *Dictionaire de Théologie Catholique* vol 2 n. 1963f.
[4.] *Christus Dominus* n.44. *The General Catechetical Directory* was the result.

Meanwhile other catechisms emerged, in particular *De Nieuwe Katechismus* from Holland in 1967 which left out considerable amounts of the Church's moral and doctrinal teaching and reinterpreted others in a way that was not orthodox. Theologians on every side echoed the words of Karl Rahner that a clear statement of faith was needed "Without this kind of a Creed the fullness of Christian faith very quickly becomes amorphous, or a believer very easily places too much value in his religious practice on things which are only secondary ... (a Christian) must have at his disposal this kind of brief formulation of his profession of faith which is orientated towards the essentials of his faith".[5]

The 1985 Synod of bishops, called to mark the twentieth anniversary of the conclusion of Vatican II expressed a desire for "a compendium or catechism of all catholic docrine to serve as a point of reference for catechisms ... in all the local churches".[6] A Commission was subsequently named by Pope John Paul, headed by Cardinal Ratzinger and began work in June 1986. A provisional text was sent out for comment to all the bishops of the Church in November 1989 and the final text published in 1992.

Although the *Catechism of the Catholic Church* follows the traditional four part format of previous catechisms, it is not a revision of them, but rather a completely new production which takes into consideration the liturgical movement, biblical research, the new appreciation of patristics and the work of Vatican II.

The inter-relation of the four parts is explained in paragraph 2558: "The Church professes her faith in the symbol of the apostles (Part I) and celebrates that faith in the liturgy (Part II), so that it might be lived out in the Church (Part III) within a personal and living relationship with God, Father, Son and Holy Spirit (Part IV)". But in facing up to contemporary problems such as drugs and family breakdown the Catechism aims to show that Catholic doctrine and moral teaching can bring unique insight and authoritative criteria to bear. It is both comprehensive and compassionate in its approach. It maintains the whole of the Church's teaching but expressed in a way that understands human weakness while presenting us with the divine mercy expressed in the love of our Saviour.

Others will develop this "symphony of the faith"[7] into catechetical programmes and local catechisms. But there is a danger that because of its very size (some 700 pages divided into 2865 paragraphs) that it will be consigned to the bookshelf or left to theologians to discusss. For this reason a *Companion and Commentary* has been

---

5. *Foundations of Christian Faith*. London 1978 p. 448.
6. "Closing Address to the Synod" 19 December, 1985.
7. *Depositum Fidei* (1992) n.2 q.v.

produced to contain all the salient points of the Catechism with elucidations for an English-speaking readership. It also includes frequent references to *Veritatis Splendor* in view of its importance for moral principles, which was issued after the publication of the Catechism. The texts consulted were the French and Spanish editions.

This is a readers' version which includes space on each page for notes. The relevant paragraph numbers of the Catechism are given in the left hand column adjacent to the text, scriptural, patristic and ecclesiastical references are placed on the opposite side.

Two appendices have been added, one giving a list of the General Councils of the Church, as there are numerous references to these in the Catechism; the second providing a selection of Catholic prayers which is more extensive than that given in the *Concise Catholic Catechism* (now in its second edition). I fervently hope that this volume will help to highlight what is basic and essential in Catholicism and encourage us all to live it in our lives and explain it to those who ask it of us.

The Oratory,   James Tolhurst
Edgbaston, Birmingham   1994

APOSTOLIC CONSTITUTION

FIDEI DEPOSITUM

ON THE PUBLICATION OF THE
CATECHISM OF THE CATHOLIC CHURCH
PREPARED FOLLOWING THE
SECOND VATICAN ECUMENICAL COUNCIL

JOHN PAUL II, BISHOP

SERVANT OF THE SERVANTS OF GOD
FOR EVERLASTING MEMORY

To my Venerable Brothers the Cardinals, to the Archbishops, Bishops, Priests, Deacons and all the People of God

1. Introduction

Guarding the deposit of faith is the mission which the Lord has entrusted to his Church and which she fulfils in every age. The Second Vatican Ecumenical Council, which was opened 30 years ago by my predecessor Pope John XXIII, of happy memory had as its intention and purpose to highlight the Church's apostolic and pastoral mission, and by making the truth of the Gospel shine forth, to lead all people to seek and receive Christ's love which surpasses all knowledge (cf. Eph 3,19).

The principal task entrusted to the Council by Pope John XXIII was to guard and present better the precious deposit of Christian doctrine in order to make it more accessible to the Christian faithful and to all people of good will. For this reason the Council was not first of all to condemn the errors of the time, but above all to strive calmly to show the strength and beauty of the doctrine of the faith. "Illumined by the light of this Council", the Pope said, "the Church ... will become greater in spiritual riches and, gaining the strength of new energies therefrom, she will look to the future without fear ... Our duty is ... to dedicate ourselves with an earnest will and without fear to that work which our era demands of us, thus pursuing the path which the Church has followed for 20 centuries".[1]

With the help of God, the Council Fathers in four years of work were able to produce a considerable collection of doctrinal statements and pastoral norms which were presented to the whole Church. There the Pastors and Christian faithful find directives for that "renewal of

---

[1]John XXIII, Opening Address to the Second Vatican Ecumenical Council, 11 October 1962: *AAS* 54 (1962), pp. 788, 791.

thought, action, practices and moral virtue, of joy and hope, which was the very purpose of the Council".[2]

After its conclusion, the Council did not cease to inspire the Church's life. In 1985 I was able to assert: "For me, then — who had the special grace of participating in it and actively collaborating in its development — Vatican II has always been, and especially during these years of my Pontificate, the constant reference point of my every pastoral action, in the conscious commitment to implement its directives concretely and faithfully at the level of each Church and the whole Church".[3]

In this spirit, on 25 January 1985 I convoked an Extraordinary Assembly of the Synod of Bishops for the 25th anniversary of the close of the Council. The purpose of this assembly was to celebrate the graces and spiritual fruits of Vatican II, to study its teaching in greater depth in order the better to adhere to it and to promote knowledge and application of it.

On that occasion the Synod Fathers stated: "Very many have expressed the desire that a catechism or compendium of all Catholic doctrine regarding both faith and morals be composed, that it might be, as it were, a point of reference for the catechisms or compendiums that are prepared in various regions. The presentation of doctrine must be biblical and liturgical. It must be sound doctrine suited to the present life of Christians".[4] After the Synod ended, I made this desire my own, considering it as "fully responding to a real need both of the universal Church and the particular Churches".[5]

For this reason we thank the Lord wholeheartedly on this day when we can offer the entire Church this "reference text" entitled the *Catechism of the Catholic Church*, for a catechesis renewed at the living sources of the faith!

Following the renewal of the Liturgy and the new codification of the canon law of the Latin Church and that of the Oriental Catholic Churches, this catechism will make a very important contribution to that work of renewing the whole life of the Church, as desired and begun by the Second Vatican Council.

---

[2]Paul VI, Closing Address to the Second Vatican Ecumenical Council, 8 December 1965: *AAS* 58 (1966), pp. 7–8

[3]John Paul II, Address of 25 January 1985: *L'Osservatore Romano*, 27 January 1985.

[4]Final Report of the Extraordinary Synod, 7 December 1985, II, B, a, n. 4: *Enchiridion Vaticanum*, vol. 9, p. 1785, n. 1797.

[5]John Paul II, Address at the closing of the Extraordinary Synod, 7 December 1985, n. 6: *AAS* 78 (1986), p. 435.

2. The process and spirit of drafting the text

The *Catechism of the Catholic Church* is the result of very extensive collaboration: it was prepared over six years of intense work done in a spirit of complete openness and fervent zeal.

In 1986 I entrusted a commission of 12 Cardinals and Bishops, chaired by Cardinal Joseph Ratzinger, with the task of preparing a draft of the catechism requested by the Synod Fathers. An editorial committee of seven diocesan Bishops, experts in theology and catechesis, assisted the commission in its work.

The commission, charged with giving directives and with overseeing the course of the work attentively followed all the stages in editing the nine subsequent drafts. The editorial committee, for its part, assumed reponsiblity for writing the text, making the emendations requested by the commission and examining the observations of numerous theologians, exegetes and catechists, and above all, of the Bishops of the whole world, in order to improve the text. The committee was a place of fruitful and enriching exchanges of opinion to ensure the unity and homegeneity of the text.

The project was the object of extensive consultation among all Catholic Bishops, their Episcopal Conferences of Synods, and of theological and catechetical institutes.[6] As a whole, it received a broadly favourable acceptance on the part of the Episcopate. It can be said that this catechism is the result of the collaboration of the whole Episcopate of the Catholic Church, who generously accepted my invitation to share responsibility for an enterprise which directly concerns the life of the Church. This response elicits in me a deep feeling of joy, because the harmony of so many voices truly expresses what could be called the "symphony" of the faith. The achievement of this catechism thus reflects the collegial nature of the Episcopate: it testifies to the Church's catholicity.

3. Arrangement of the material

A catechism should faithfully and systematically present the teaching of Sacred Scripture, the living Tradition of the Church and the authentic Magisterium, as well as the spiritual heritage of the Fathers and the Church's saints, to allow for a better knowledge of the Christian mystery and for enlivening the faith of the People of God. It should take into account the doctrinal statements which down the centuries the Holy Spirit has intimated to his Church. It should also help illumine with the light of faith the new situations and problems which had not yet emerged in the past.

---

[6] 20,000 amendments were received by the editorial committee

The catechism will thus contain the new and the old (cf. Mt 13,52), because the faith is always the same yet the source of ever new light.

To respond to this twofold demand, the *Catechism of the Catholic Church* on the one hand repeats the "old", traditional order already followed by the Catechism of St Pius V, arranging the material in four parts: the *Creed, the Sacred Liturgy,* with pride of place given to the Sacraments, the *Christian way of life,* explained beginning with the Ten Commandments, and finally, *Christian prayer.* At the same time, however, the contents are often expressed in a "new" way in order to respond to the questions of our age.

The four parts are related one to the other: the Christian mystery is the object of faith (first part); it is celebrated and communicated in liturgical actions (second part); it is present to enlighten and sustain the children of God in their actions (third part); it is the basis for our prayer, the privileged expression of which is the *Our Father,* and it represents the object of our supplication, our praise and our intercession (fourth part).

The Liturgy itself is prayer; the confession of faith finds its proper place in the celebration of worship. Grace, the fruit of the sacraments, is the irreplaceable condition for Christian living, just as participation in the Church's liturgy requires faith. If faith is not expressed in works, it is dead (cf. Jas 2, 14 – 16) and cannot bear fruit unto eternal life.

In reading the *Catechism of the Catholic Church* we can perceive the wondrous unity of the mystery of God, his saving will, as well as the central place of Jesus Christ, the only-begotten Son of God, sent by the Father, made man in the womb of the Blessed Virgin Mary by the power of the Holy Spirit, to be our Saviour. Having died and risen, Christ is always present in his Church, especially in the sacraments; he is the source of our faith, the model of Christian conduct and the teacher of our prayers.

4. The doctrinal value of the text

The *Catechism of the Catholic Church,* which I approved 25 June last and the publication of which I today order by virtue of the Church's faith and of Catholic doctrine, attested to or illumined by Sacred Scripture, Apostolic Tradition and the Church's Magisterium. I declare it to be a valid and legitimate instrument for ecclesial communion and a sure norm for teaching the faith. May it serve the renewal to which the Holy Spirit ceaselessly calls the Church of God, the Body of Christ, on her pilgrimage to the undiminished light of the kingdom!

The approval and publication of the *Catechism of the Catholic Church* represents a service which the Successor of Peter wishes to offer to the Holy Catholic Church, and to all the particular Churches in peace and communion with the Apostolic See: the service, that is, of supporting and confirming the faith of all the Lord Jesus' disciples (cf. Lk 22,32), as well as of strengthening the bonds of unity in the same apostolic faith.

Therefore, I ask the Church's Pastors and the Christian faithful to receive this catechism in a spirit of communion and to use it assiduously in fulfilling their mission of proclaiming the faith and calling people to the Gospel life. This catechism is given to them that it may be a sure and authentic reference text for teaching Catholic doctrine and particularly for preparing local catechisms. It is also offered to all the faithful who wish to deepen their knowledge of the unfathomable riches of salvation (cf. Jn 8:32). It is meant to support ecumenical efforts that are moved by the holy desire for the unity of all Christians, showing carefully the content of wondrous harmony of the Catholic faith. The *Catechism of the Catholic Church*, lastly, is offered to every individual who asks us to give an account of the hope that is in us (cf. 1 Pt 3, 15) and who wants to know what the Catholic Church believes.

This catechism is not intended to replace the local catechisms duly approved by the ecclesiastical authorities, the diocesan Bishops and Episcopal Conferences, especially if they have been approved by the Apostolic See. It is meant to encourage and assist in the writing of new local catechisms, which must take into account various situations and cultures, while carefully preserving the unity of faith and fidelity to Catholic doctrine.

5. Conclusion

At the conclusion of this document presenting the *Catechism of the Catholic Church*, I beseech the Blessed Virgin Mary, Mother of the Incarnate Word and Mother of the Church, to support with her powerful intercession the catechetical work of the entire Church on every level, at this time when she is called to a new effort of evangelization. May the light of the true faith free humanity from ignorance and slavery to sin in order to lead it to the only freedom worthy of the name (cf. Jn 8,32): that of life in Jesus Christ under the guidance of the Holy Spirit, here below and in the kingdom of heaven, in the fulness of the blessed vision of God face to face (cf. 1 Cor 13, 12, 2 Cor 5, 6–)!

Given on 11 October 1992, the thirtieth anniversary of the opening of the Second Vatican Ecumenical Council, in the fourteenth year of my Pontificate.

Joannes Paulus Pp II

Part One

The Profession of Faith

Section I   I Believe, We Believe

Chapter 1: Man is capable of attaining God

27   Man is created by God and therefore has the desire for God implanted in him, together with a yearning for goodness and truth. God draws man to himself and man in turn searches to satisfy his longing.

GS 19

28   This search for God has found different expressions in prayer, sacrifice, worship and meditation, which however confused, can be found throughout history in every culture, and convince us that man is a religious being.

Acts 16, 26-28

29   Yet man can forget his link with God or even reject it. This can be due to ignorance or religious indifference, alternatively it can be due to depression caused by the cares of the world and the delight in riches, the bad example of believers, depressed by all the evil to be found in the world, the influence of those who are hostile to religion, or finally because man, being a sinner, hides from God and runs away from him.

Mt 13,22

Gen 3,10
Jon 1,3

31   Man comes to a knowledge of the existence of God through convincing and convergent arguments ('Proofs for the Existence of God') which allow him to reach certainty. These can be divided into proofs from Creation and proofs from human nature itself.

Aug Conf 1,1,1

Aquinas
S T I,2

32   The world leads us to the concept of a Creator. Let us only consider the idea of movement and change, the order and beauty of the world and its contingent nature.

Rom 1,19−20
Acts 14,15f;
17, 27−8
Wis 13,1−9
Aug Ser 24

33 Man himself possesses a sense of what is right and good. This sense, along with his freedom and his conscience urge him towards the infinite and lasting happiness. All of this argues to the existence of the spiritual soul which can only be explained by God.

GS 18.1
cf. 14,2

The teaching of the Church

36 The Church teaches that 'God, the origin and end of all things, can be known with certainty by the natural light of human reason from the things that he created'. Man has this capacity because he is made in God's image; without that it would be impossible to come to any knowledge of God.

Vatican I
DS 3004

37 But although human reason is truly capable of attaining a true and certain knowledge of God, there are many obstacles which prevent man using this faculty effectively, for we are entering a realm that totally transcends the visible order and demands of human beings a measure of self-sacrifice and humility. At the same time there is the impact on the imagination of the consequences of original sin, which introduce confusion into the mind and heart.

Pius XII
HG
DS 3876

38 A knowledge of God which is based on solid certainty with no trace of error demands Divine revelation, not only because it surpasses human understanding, but also because such revelation is morally necessary to understand religious and moral truths connected with our knowledge of God.

Vatican I
DS 3005
Pius XII
HG
DS 3876

39 When we talk about God, who we believe is at the heart of our dialogue with other religions, we recognise that he transcends every creature. Our words are therefore limited because 'between the Creator and the creature we can notice no similarity so great that a greater dissimilarity cannot be seen between them' and because we cannot grasp what God is in himself, but only what he is not and how other beings are placed in relation to him.

Wis 13,5

Lat IV
DS 806
Aquinas
C G
1,30

Chapter 2: God goes out to meet mankind

50   There is another way by which man can know God, which surpasses his own powers and is known as divine *Revelation*. God reveals himself and gives himself to man by a totally free decision on his part.

Vatican I
DS 3015

51   God dwells in unapproachable light (I Tim 6,16), but wants to share his divine life with those who have been freely created, so that they can become his adopted children in his only Son (cf. Eph 1,4–5). He desires that men might become capable of responding to him, of knowing him and loving him in a way that is beyond their own natural capabilities.

DV 2

53   This God accomplished in stages as our divine teacher, revealing his plan step by step so that mankind could finally receive that Revelation which culminated in the Person and mission of the Incarnate Word Jesus Christ.

DV 2
Irenaeus 5
A H
3,20,2

54   This Revelation began with our first parents who were invited to enter into communion with Him and were filled with grace and holiness, which was not abandoned when they sinned, but was accompanied with the promise of redemption and a renewal of the covenant between God and man. We see this take place with Noah after the flood, and through him, with the nations. This all embracing plan of God which is entrusted to the care of the guardian angels, is designed to curb that innate pride which likes to erect its tower of Babel and turn towards poytheism and idolatry nonetheless it endures through such universal just men, as Abel, Melchisedech (a figure of the Messiah), Daniel and Job, looking forward to that day when Christ 'would gather into one the children of God who are scattered abroad' (Jn 11,52)

DV 3
MR EP IV.
118

Gen 10,5
Acts 17,
26–27.

Lk 21,24

Gen 14,18
Ez 14,14

God called Abraham 'from his country, and his kindred and his father's house', (Gen 12,1) so that

Gen 11,4

he could gather together that scattered humanity to make of him 'the father of a multitude of nations' (Gen 17,5) in whom all the nations would be blessed. The people of Abraham would inherit the promise and the call to prepare for that gathering of all the children of God into the unity of the Church. They would be the stock on to which the shoot of the believing gentiles would be grafted.

Eph 3,8
Rom 11,28
Jn 11,52
Rom,11,17f

61   The patriarchs and prophets, the Kings and wise men, have been and always will be venerated as saints in the liturgical traditions of the Church. After these patriarchs, God formed his people Israel, saving them from slavery in Egypt. He sealed a covenant with them on Sinai and through Moses gave the law, so that they could serve him, the only God, living and true, merciful Father and just judge, in joyful hope of the new and eternal covenant. The prophets looked forward to that fullness of redemption and the forgiveness of all iniquity which would embrace all nations. That hope was kept alive especially in those holy women of the Scriptures, Sarah, Rebecca, Rachel, Miriam, Deborah, Anne, Judith and Esther and that most pure Virgin of Nazareth, Mary.

Is 2,2–4
Jer 31,
31–34
Ez 36,8–11
Is 49,5–6

Lk 1,38

65   'In many and various ways God spoke of old to our fathers by the prophets; but in these last days he has spoken to us by a Son' (Heb 1,1–2). Christ is that unique, perfect and unsurpassable Word of the Father. In him he has said everything and there will never be another word to say. The new Covenant is final and will not pass away, nor will there be any new revelation until the glorious coming of our Saviour on the clouds of heaven; but revelation remains to be made fully explicit down through the centuries. Private revelations should only be accepted if they do not correct or go beyond divine Revelation, but rather help us to live our faith more deeply and help our devotion 'do not despise prophesying, but test everything; hold fast to what is good' (I Thes 5, 29).

John of
Cross
Carm 2,22
DV 4

The transmission of Revelation

74 God 'desires all men to be saved and to come to the knowledge of the truth' (I Tim 2,4), that is to say, Jesus Christ (cf. Jn 14,6). This means that Christ must be preached to all mankind even to the ends of the world.   DV 7

76 The Gospel is handed on according to the Lord's command either *orally* or *in writing*, under the inspiration of the Holy Spirit, by the apostles and their companions. Their successors, the bishops, faithfully continue that apostolic preaching which is especially expressed in the inspired books of the New Testament until the end of time. There is a close link between the transmission of this preaching (which is called *Tradition*) and Holy Scripture which is the written word. We need to remember that the Father who communicates Himself through his Word in the Holy Spirit, remains actively present in the Church.   DV 7 DV 8 DV 9 DV 8

81 *Tradition*, which comes from the apostles, transmits the teaching and example which they received from Jesus through the power of the Holy Spirit. The first Christians relied on that living tradition which gave rise to the New Testament itself

84 The *Deposit of faith* (cf I Tim 6,20) which is contained in Sacred Tradition and Holy Scripture, has been committed by the apostles to the whole Church. But the task of interpreting the Word of God has been given to the *Magisterium* or Teaching Authority of the Church, the bishops in communion with the successor of Peter, the Bishop of Rome, who teach in Christ's name and faithfully hand on through the assistance of the Holy Spirit the word of God. The faithful people of God must receive their teaching with humble acceptance (cf Lk 10,16). This is especially true when the Magisterium defines *dogmas* : truths contained in divine Revelation or truths which have a necessary connection with Revelation relating to faith or morals. Dogmas are intimately connected to our spiritual life. They clarify and   2 Tim 1, 12–14.   DV 10 DV 10

strengthen our faith and if we live our faith to the full, our mind and heart will be open to accept the dogmas which are taught (cf I Jn 2,20,27). The interaction between the various dogmas and the foundation of the faith itself gives rise to 'a hierarchy of truths'.

VS 4.26

Vatican I
DS 3016

UR 11

91   The whole body of the faithful receiving the word of God, have a supernatural grasp of the truth, which does not lead them into error, as they remain united to their bishops. There is thus a growth or development of the faith which takes place through contemplation and research, by spiritual appreciation of the words and by the preaching of the bishops themselves, so that the Magisterium, Tradition and Holy Scripture are closely interlinked through the action of the Holy Spirit at work in the Church.

LG 12
DV 8
GS 62

DV 10

Holy Scripture

101   God has only spoken one Word, his only Son, in whom he said all that can be said. For this reason the Church venerates the Scriptures as she venerates the Lord's own Body. It is also the case that our heavenly Father comes to us with all tenderness and shares his thoughts with us. God is the author of Scripture, inspiring the human authors to express divine truth faithfully and without error, but we depend upon the Holy Spirit and Christ, the Eternal Word of the Living God, so that it may live in our hearts and minds.

Heb 1,1–3

Aug
Ps 103,4,1

DV 21.24
DV 11
Lk 24,45

109   God speaks to mankind using human authors and therefore it is necessary to discover what the writers really meant and what God wanted to reveal to us through their words; we need to bear in mind the narrative conventions prevailing at the time, and the literary forms made use of by the author (i.e. poetical, prophetic or historical).

DV 12

111   Vatican II has given us *three criteria* to enable us to interpret Scripture with the divine authorship in mind:
    1. The content and unity of the whole of Scripture.

DV 12

Although there is a manifest diversity between various books of the Scriptures, there is a unity in God's plan, of which Jesus is the centre as he made clear after his Resurrection (Lk 24, 25–27.44–46)

Aquinas
Ps 21,11
Aquinas
ST I,1,10

2. Scripture must be read within the living tradition of the Church. The Church has within its Tradition, the living memory of the Word of God, prompting under the inspiration of the Holy Spirit the spiritual meaning of Scripture.

3. Taking into account the 'analogy of faith'. By 'analogy of faith' we understand the mutual interrelation of the truths of faith comprising the whole of Revelation.

cf Rom
12,6

The meaning of Scripture

116 1. *The literal meaning*

The meaning of the words discovered by the exegete using the standard rules of interpretation. 'All meanings of Holy Scripture rest on the literal sense'.

Aquinas
ST I,1,10

117 2. *The spiritual meaning*

Not simply the text itself, but also the events themselves and the realities described can signify some deeper reality; thus Melchisedech is a figure of Christ (Heb 7,3).

a) Allegorical meaning
We can gain a deeper understanding of the events described by seeing them related to the life of Christ; the crossing of the Red Sea can be seen as a sign of the victory of Christ, and beyond that of baptism.

I Cor 10,2

b) Moral meaning
The events recorded are written 'for our instruction' (I Cor 10,11)

Heb 3–4,11

c) Anagogical meaning

The realities and events are seen in the context of eternity, leading (*anagoge*) us towards our home in heaven; the Church is the sign of the heavenly Jerusalem (Apo 21,1–22,5).

119   Everything concerning the manner of interpreting Scripture is ultimately subject to the judgement of the Church which has the divine mandate to safeguard the word of God and interpret it. S. Augustine writes that he would not believe in the Gospel unless the authority of the Catholic Church urged him to.   Fund 5,6

The canon of Scripture

120   Apostolic Tradition has aided the Church to discern which writings should be numbered among the *Canon* (List) of Scripture. There are 46 writings (45 if Jeremiah and Lamentations are counted as one book) in the Old Testament and 27 in the New:
Genesis, Exodus, Leviticus, Numbers, Deuteronomy, Joshua, Judges, Ruth, I and II Samuel, I and II Kings, I and II Chronicles, Esdras, Nehemiah, Tobit, Judith, Esther, I and II Maccabees, Job, Psalms, Proverbs, Ecclesiastes, Song of Solomon, Wisdom, Sirach*, Isaiah, Jeremiah, Lamentations, Baruch, Ezekiel, Daniel, Hoseah, Joel, Amos, Obadiah, Jonah, Micah, Nahum, Habakkuk, Zephaniah, Haggai, Zechariah, Malachi. (The Old Testament)
The Gospel according to Matthew, Mark, Luke and John, the Acts of the Apostles, the Epistles of S. Paul to the Romans, I and II Corinthians, Galatians, Ephesians, Philippians, Colossians, I and II Thessalonians, I and II to Timothy, Titus, Philemon, The Epistle to the Hebrews, James, I and II Peter, I, II and III John, The Epistle of Jude, Apocalypse or Revelation. (The New Testament)

---

*or Ecclesiasticus

The Old Testament

121 The Old Testament is an essential part of Holy
Scripture. Its books are divinely inspired and have
a permanent value because the Old Covenant *has
never been revoked* (denied by *Marcion*, the   DV 14
second century heretic) and is part of the divine
plan leading to Christ.   DV 15

The New Testament

124 The writings of the New Testament provide us   DV 17
with the fullness of divine Revelation, centred on
Christ, the Son of the Incarnate God, his acts, his
teachings, his passion and his resurrection, as well
as the beginnings of the Church.   DV20

126 We can see three stages in the formation of the
Gospels:

a) The life and teaching of Jesus
The Church firmly believes that the four Gospels
hand down to us faithfully what Jesus, the Son of
God truly said and taught during his life on earth,
until the day when he was taken up into heaven.

b) Oral tradition
All that the Lord said and did was handed on by
the apostles after his Ascension, to their listeners
with that profound understanding which they
possessed, having been instructed by the glorified
Lord and enlightened by the Holy Spirit of Truth.

c) The written Gospels
The evangelists composed the four Gospels,
choosing certain items which had been
remembered orally or recorded in writing, making
syntheses of others or explaining certain things in
connection with a particular Church situation,
making use of the form of preaching, in such a
way as to give us always a true and sincere account
about the Person of Jesus Christ.   DV 19

127 The Gospels have always had a unique place in the
Church, as witnessed by the veneration accorded

to them by the liturgy and the attraction they have
exercised on the saints in every age.

The unity of Scripture

128   The Church has had recourse to *typology* from
apostolic times, and subsequently in her
Tradition, to see the unity of God's plan in the
two Testaments. This enables her to see the works
of God accomplished in the Old Testament as
prefiguring what will take place in the fullness of
time in the Son of God. Christians who read the
Old Testament in the light of Christ crucified and
risen and cannot forget that its value as
Revelation was reaffirmed by our Lord himself
(cf Mk 12,29–31). Thus it is said that the New is
hidden in the Old and in the New the Old is
revealed.

I Cor 10,
6.11

Heb 10,1

I Pt 3,21

Aug
Hept 2,73

133   The Church advises Christians that they will
acquire through frequent reading of Scripture
surpassing knowledge of Jesus Christ (Phil 3,8)
because, according to S. Jerome, to ignore the
Scriptures is to ignore Christ.

Comm in
Is Prol.

Chapter 3: The response man makes to God

142   God invites mankind to enter into communion
with him by means of his revelation. This demands on our part the complete *homage of faith*.
We talk about *homage*, because we freely submit
to the word we hear. This is because God is the
guarantor who cannot deceive us. Abraham is put
forward as a model of faith, and Our Lady as the
most perfect example of faithful response.

DV 2.5

Vatican I
DS 3008

145   We are told that 'By faith Abraham obeyed when
he was called to go out to a place which he was to
receive as an inheritance and he went out, not
knowing where he was to go' (Heb 11,8). By faith
he lived as a stranger and wanderer in the
promised land (Gen 23,4) and by faith 'Sarah
herself received power to conceive' the son she had
been promised (Heb 11,11) whom Abraham

offered up (Heb 11,17). Because he had that powerful faith (Rom 4,20) he became the 'father of all those who believed' (Rom 4,11,18) But in spite of the many witnesses to faith given us in the Scriptures 'God had foreseen something better for us' (Heb 11,40), the grace of believing in his Son, 'the pioneer and perfecter of our faith' (Heb 12,2).

148 The Virgin Mary welcomed the message of the angel Gabriel, believing that 'nothing is impossible for God' (Lk 1,37) and gave her wiling consent   Gen 18,14
'Behold, I am the handmaid of the Lord; let it be to me according to your word' (Lk 1,38). Her cousin   Lk 1,45
Elizabeth praised her faith and indeed all generations call her blessed (Lk 1,48). That faith did not waver even as she stood beneath the Cross, believing in the accomplishment of the word of God which pierced her heart with sorrow.   Lk 2,35

'I know whom I have believed'   2 Tim 1,12

150 Faith is mankind's personal attachment of God   Jer 17,5−6
and his free assent to what God has revealed. But for the Christian this involves believing in the   Ps 40,5;
beloved Son in whom He is well pleased (Mk   146,3−4
1,11). We cannot in fact see God unless the only Son 'who is in the bosom of the Father' makes him known. Yet it is the Holy Spirit who reveals Jesus   Jn 14,1
to us, because the Spirit searches even the depths   Jn 1,18;
of God and no one can say 'Jesus is Lord' except   6,46
by the Holy Spirit. Therefore the Church   I Cor
professes her faith in one God, Father, Son and   2,10−11
Holy Spirit.   I Cor 12,3

Characteristics of faith

153 Faith is a gift of God, a supernatural virtue infused by him. It was for this reason that Jesus declared to S. Peter that he was the Christ, the Son of the living God the revelation 'had not come from flesh and blood, but from my Father who is in heaven' (Mt 16,17). It is not possible to believe without grace and the interior assistance of the Holy Spirit, but this does not make an act of faith

any less human. It is neither contrary to man's freedom nor to his intelligence for man to put his trust in God and believe in what he has revealed. We do not regard it as somehow demeaning to trust the intentions or promises which are made to us on the human level, for instance in marriage, far less should it be beneath our dignity to give the homage of our intelligence and will to God who reveals himself.

GS 17
Aquinas
ST 2–2,
2,9.

V S 42

Faith and intellect

156   Ultimately we believe 'because of the authority of God Himself who can neither deceive nor be deceived'; but God, together with the assistance of the Holy Spirit which we receive interiorly, also gives us exterior proofs of the validity of his revelation by means of the miracles of Christ and the saints, prophecies, and the very growth and holiness of the Church itself. Although the truths of revelation may appear hard to fathom, we can put our complete faith in them, however much we may hesitate, because 'ten thousand difficulties do not make one doubt'. In fact it is the nature of faith that we should desire to understand more, because the greater our knowledge, the greater will be our faith, and so will be our love; the grace of faith enlightening the eyes of our heart (Eph 1,18).

Vatican I
3008–10;
3013

Mk 16,20
Heb 2,4
Aquinas
ST
2–2,171,5

Newman
Apo p.6

Anselm
Prosl.
Proem.

Aug
Hom 43,7

159   There is no contradiction between the mysteries of faith and the discoveries of science, because what is true in one sphere can never conflict with truth found in any other sphere. Both have their source in God, who directs the hand of those who with perseverance and humility seek to unlock the mysteries of science.

Vatican I
DS 3017

GS 36

Faith and conscience

160   God calls man to serve him in spirit and truth, which demands that it should be freely given. One cannot force people to believe, even though once man receives the call of God, he is obliged in conscience to accept the weight of that responsibility, because belief in God and in the

Christ he has sent is necessary for salvation, and
we must ask that we might persevere in faith to
the end, so as to obtain eternal life (Mt 10,22;
24,13; I Tim 1,18–19)

Vatican I
DS 3012
Trent
DS 1532

'Look, Lord on the faith of your Church'

168   In the *Roman Ritual* the minister of baptism asks
the catechumen 'What do you ask of the
Church?' and the reply is, 'Faith'. 'What does
faith give you?' 'Eternal life'. Salvation comes to
us from the Church which believes, feeds and
sustains our faith, and which confesses in the *Te
Deum* the Lordship of God throughout the
universe. We believe in the Church as the mother
of our new birth and the one who instructs us in
our faith.

Faustus of
Riez
Spir 1,2

The formulations of Faith

170   There is a sense in which language fails in the
presence of the mystery of God, 'Though we
speak much we cannot reach the end, and the sum
of our words is: "He is the all"' (Sir 43,27). But
dogmatic formulae do convey to us the meaning
of revealed truth 'which was once and for all
delivered to the saints' (Jude 3). New presenta-
tions of doctrine must retain that permanent
meaning even as they express it in a new way.

Vatican I
DS 3020

ME 5

The Creed or Credo

The Apostles' Creed or Symbol of the Apostles	The Niceno-Constantinopolitan Creed
I believe in God, the Father almighty, creator of heaven and earth.	I believe in one God, the Father almighty, creator of heaven and earth, of all things, both visible and invisible.
I believe in Jesus Christ, his only Son, our Lord.	And in one Lord Jesus Christ, the only begotten Son of God, born of the Father before all time; light from light, true God from true God; begotten not created, consubstantial with the Father; through him all things were made. For the sake of us men and for our salvation, he came down from heaven,
He was conceived by the power of the Holy Spirit and born of the Virgin Mary. He suffered under Pontius Pilate, was crucified, died, and was buried. He descended to the dead. On the third day he rose again.	was made flesh by the Holy Spirit from the Virgin Mary, and became man; and he was crucified for our sake under Pontius Pilate, suffered and was buried. And on the third day he arose according to the Scriptures;
He ascended into heaven, and is seated at the right hand of the Father. He will come again to judge the living and the dead	he ascended into heaven sits at the right hand of the Father, and is going to come again in glory to judge the living and the dead. His reign will have no end.
I believe in the Holy Spirit,	I believe in the Holy Spirit, the Lord, the giver of life; he proceeds from the Father, is adored and honoured together with the Father and the Son; he spoke through the prophets.
the holy Catholic Church,	I believe in one, holy, Catholic, and apostolic Church. the communion of saints,
the forgiveness of sins,	I profess one baptism for the forgiveness of sins,
the resurrection of the body, and the life everlasting. Amen.	I expect the resurrection of the dead and the life of the world to come. Amen.

Section II The Creed

The Christian profession of faith & the Symbols of faith

185 Whoever says 'I believe' is saying in fact 'I accept what *we* believe'. That communion in the one faith demands a common expression of faith, binding on all and uniting everyone in the same confession of faith.

186 The apostolic community expressed and handed on its faith in short formulae, but it was also found necessary to provide summaries of the faith, especially in connection with candidates being prepared for baptism [catechumens]. These syntheses of faith were known as *Creeds,* because they normally began with the Latin 'I believe' or *Symbols*, the Greek word for collection or summary.

Rom 10,9
I Cor 15,3f

Cyril
Cat 5,12

189 The Symbol of faith connected with baptism distinguishes the three Persons of the Trinity: 'Firstly there is the question of the first divine Person and the wonderful work of creation; then of the second divine Person and the mystery of mankind's redemption; lastly of the third divine Person, source and principal of our sanctification.' These three parts, distinct but interconnected, came to be known as *articles*, and gradually this become the name given to the various truths of faith. By the time of S. Ambrose they had become the twelve articles of the faith, symbolizing the apostolic faith of the twelve apostles.

RC
I,1,3

Symb 5

192 The most famous of these symbols are: *Quicunque*, attributed to S. Athanasius; the professions of the Councils: Toledo, Lateran, Lyons, Trent; or those of the Popes; the Profession of faith of Pope Damasus, and latterly, the *Credo of the People of God* of Pope Paul VI in 1968. Two have an outstanding place in the life of the Church, the *Apostle's Creed*, the

DS 75 – 6
DS 525 – 41
800 – 2;851
861;1862 –
70;71 – 2.

profession of faith used for catechumens by the Church of Rome, and the *Niceno-Constantino-politan* (or *Nicene*) creed which was compiled as a result of the Councils of Nicea (325) and Constantinople (381). The Catechism follows the text of the Apostle's Creed but completes this from time to time with reference to the more elaborate Nicene Creed.

Chapter 1 Belief in God the Father Almighty, Creator of Heaven and Earth

'I believe in one God'

200   The Nicene Creed begins in this way, reminding us that our faith in rooted in the faith of the Covenant of Israel which acknowledged that there was only one God, who must be loved with their whole heart and soul and strength. This faith was confirmed by Jesus (cf Mk 12,29–30) referring to the Lord their God. Belief in the Trinity in no way affects our belief in the oneness of God who is eternal, infinite, unchangeable and almighty, three Persons indeed, but of one essence, substance or nature which is entirely simple.

Dt 6,4–5
Is 45,22–24
Phil 2,10f

Lat IV
DS 800

God reveals his name

203   The revealing of a name in ancient times was a disclosure of the mystery of one's inner self and life to others. God did not wish to remain an anonymous power, but rather someone who was accessible and capable of being known and loved. He revealed himself progressively and under different names, but the most significant revelation was made to Moses at the burning bush, where he spoke to him from the midst of the fire to tell him that He was the God of his ancestors, who was faithful to his promises and looked with compassion on the suffering of his people whom he would deliver from slavery. Moses replied to God, 'If I come to the people of Israel and say to

them, "The God of your fathers has sent me to
you", and they ask me, "What is his name?" what
shall I say to them?' God said to Moses, 'I AM WHO
I AM' and he said 'This is what you will say to the
people of Israel, "I am" has sent me to you ...
this is my name for ever, and thus I am to be
remembered throughout all generations'. (Ex
3,13–15). The almost cryptic nature of the divine   Ex 3,6
name YHWH reveals to us that God is always
present to his people as their saviour, and yet at
the same time remains a hidden God (Is 45,15)
whose name is ineffable (Jdg 13,18). Before him
Moses felt that great awe in the presence of the   Ex 3,12
Holy One, as did Isaiah who cried out 'Woe is me!   Ex 3,5–6
For I am lost; for I am a man of unclean lips', for   Is 6,5
truly He is the Holy One in our midst, before   Hos 11,9
whom we are all aware of our sinfulness.   Lk 5,8

209   The people of Israel had such reverence for the
name of God that they used in its place the title
Adonai (kyrios) 'Lord' which would later be
applied to Jesus, as in I Cor 12,3 and in '*Lord*,
have mercy' at Mass.

211   The divine name also expresses the fidelity of God
who is 'slow to anger and rich in mercy' who   Ex 34,5–6
listens to the intercession of Moses and does not   Ex 32
abandon those who abandoned him to worship   Ex 33,12f
the golden calf, but is ready to pardon them,
keeping steadfast love to the thousandth
generation. God reveals the extent of his mercy   Eph 2,4
when he delivers up his only Son, and in the gift of
his life, Jesus makes claim to the divine name
'when you have lifted up the Son of man, then you
will know that "I am"'. (Jn 8,28 Greek text)

God alone IS

214   '*I am who I am*' contains that understanding of
the truth that God alone IS. There are no other   Is 44,6
gods apart from him and he transcends the world
and time, for the heavens are the work of his
hands: 'They will perish but you will remain. They
will all wear out like a garment ... but you neither
change nor come to an end.' (Ps 102, 27–28).

God is therefore the fullness of Being, and
perfection, without beginning or end. He alone is
his own being and gives being to all that exists.   Jas 1,17

He Who Is, is Truth and Love

214   God revealed himself in his works as abounding in
steadfast love and faithfulness. God is Truth
itself, and his words are founded on truth, for in
him there is no darkness. As eternal Wisdom,
who ordered the heavens and the earth, the truth
of each thing can be seen in relation to Him. When   Ex 34,6
he sends his Son into the world, it is to bear   Ps 119,
witness to the truth, and we know that the Son of   160
God has come because 'He has given us   I Jn 1,5
understanding that we may know him who is true'   Mal 2,6
(1Jn 5,20).   Jn 18,37

218   But S. John will declare that the very being of   I Jn 4,8.1
God is love. Israel could discover that the reason   Dt 4,37
for everything that God did was found in   Hos 11,1
merciful and boundless love which could be   Is 49,14ff
compared with the love of a father for his son, or   Is 62,4−5
a mother for her children, or a spouse for his   Jn 3,16
beloved. It would even show itself in the ultimate   Jn 13,1
gift, who having loved His own in the world,
loved them to the end. In sending his only Son
and the Holy Spirit, God reveals that He is
himself an eternal exchange of love, in which we   I Cor 2,7
are destined to share.   Eph 3,9f

The significance of faith in one God

222   This article of our faith has tremendous
consequences for the whole of our life:

* We can understand the greatness and the
majesty of God, for he exceeds all our   Job 36,26
knowledge, and is worthy of our homage.
* Our whole life should be a thanksgiving, for all
that we are and all that we have comes from   I Cor 4,7
Him 'What are you that you have not   Ps 116,12
received?'
* We can know the true dignity of every person,   Gen 1,26
for all are made in the image of God.

* It enables us to use created things properly, Mt 5,29–30
because we see everything in relation to our 16,24;19,23
service of God.

* We have trust in God always, even in adversity.

'The Father'

'In the name of the Father, and of the Son and of
the Holy Spirit'

The Father revealed by the Son

238 God is called 'Father' in many religions – the
divinity is often known as father of gods and men.
Israel addresses God as Father, because he is Dt 32,6
Creator of the world. He is also known as father Mal 2,10
because of the law and covenant with Israel 'his
first born' (Ex 4,22) and is especially father of the
poor, the orphan, and defender of the widow (Ps
27,10). But Jesus reveals that God is father in a
unique sense. He is not simply father being Creator,
He is eternally Father in relation to his only Son, Jn 1,1
who is Son because of his relation to his Father: Col 1,15
'No one knows the Son except the Father, and no Heb 1,3
one knows the Father except the Son and those to
whom the Son chooses to reveal Him.' (Mt 11,27)
The Nicene Creed expresses this relationship by
using the term *consubstantial*, or 'one in being'
and the second Ecumenical Council at Constantinople in 381 confessed that Jesus Christ was 'the
only-begotten Son of God, engendered from the
Father before all ages, Light from Light, true God
from true God, begotten not made, consubstantial (*homoousios*) with the Father'. DS 150

The use of the word *Father* in reference to God is
a parental image because our parents are the first
images we receive when we come into the world;
but God is above fatherhood (and motherhood –
cf Is 66,13; Ps 131,2) because he is neither man nor
woman, but God and nobody is Father as God is
father.

The Father and the Son revealed by the Spirit

243 The Holy Spirit present at the dawn of creation Gen 1,2
and speaking through the prophets was sent at

Pentecost to be 'another Paraclete' (= Advocate)   Jn 14,17
who would dwell with the disciples and be with
them to teach them and to lead them to the
fullness of truth.   Jn 16,13

244   The eternal origin of the Spirit is revealed in his
mission in time, being sent to the apostles and the   Jn 16,14
Church by the Father in the name of the Son and   Jn 14,26
by the Son himself from the Father's side after his   Jn 15,26
resurrection. The Church therefore professes her
faith in the Holy Spirit, Lord and giver of life who
proceeds from the Father, but is linked in-   Creed
separably with the Son; 'for the Third Person of   Nic-Con
the Trinity is God, one and equal with God the   DS 150
Father and God the Son, of one substance as well
as of one nature ... He is called the Spirit not   Tol
only of the Father nor of the Son but equally of   DS 527
the Father and of the Son'. The Council of
Florence declared in 1439 that 'The Holy Spirit is
entirely in the Father and the Son and eternally
proceeds from both, as from one principle and
through one spiration ... and since everything
that belongs to the Father, he has through
generation given to his only begotten Son, except
being Father, so the Son has eternally from the
Father, by whom he was eternally begotten, that   Flo
the Holy Spirit also proceeds from the Son   DS 1300 –
eternally.'   1301

246   The affirmation of the procession of the Holy   DS 284
Spirit from the Father *and* the Son (*filioque*) can
be traced to S. Leo in 447. It entered the liturgy
from the eighth century onwards and remains a
bone of contention between Rome and the Eastern
Churches. The Orthodox confess that the Holy   AG 2
Spirit proceeds from the Father *through* the Son.
The Roman tradition says that its expression
emphasises that the Father is the source who has
no beginning, although there is only one principle
and a single spiration. The two explanations can   DS 1331
be seen as complementary.   DS 850

The Holy Trinity

Formulation of the Dogma

249   The revelation of the Trinity was expressed in the
early Church in its baptismal faith and practice, in   2 Cor 13,13
its preaching, prayer and catechesis as well as in its
Eucharistic liturgy. Gradually the Church needed
to deepen its understanding of this central truth of
faith, particularly in the face of error and this was
the work of the early Councils which drew on
philosophical terms to explain the dogma.

251   The term *substance* (or essence, or nature =
ousia) is used to explain the unity of the divine
being; *person* or *hypostasis* distinguishes the
Father, the Son and the Holy Spirit in terms of
their *relation* with each other.

The Dogma

253   * *The Trinity is One.* There are not three gods,
but one God in three persons, 'The consubstantial Trinity'. The divine persons do not
share the one divinity but each of them is God.   DS 421

* *The divine persons are really distinct from
each other*. Father, Son and Holy Spirit are
not ways of expressing the divine. They are
distinct by reason of their *relation* to each   Lat IV
other.   DS 804

* *The divine persons differ only in their relation
to each other*. 'These Three Persons are one   Tol
God ... and everything in them is one where   DS 528
there is no opposition of relationship'.   Flo
DS 1330

The Divine Works and Trinitarian Missions

257   The whole of the divine *economy* is the common
work of the three divine Persons because as there
is only one and the same nature, so there is only
one and the same operation : 'the Father, the Son
and the Holy Spirit are not three principles of   Flo
creation but one'. So we sing in the hymn at   DS 1331
vespers, 'O Trinity, blessed light, primeval
Unity'.

258   Each divine Person works according to his personal way of action, and so the Church professes her faith in 'one God and Father from whom are all things, and one Lord Jesus Christ, through whom are all things, and one Holy Spirit in whom are all things'. The whole of the Christian life is an invitation to communion with the unity of the Blessed Trinity: 'If anyone loves me, he will keep my word', says the Lord, 'and my Father will love him and we will come to him and make our home with him' (Jn 14,23). Const II
DS 421

Economy is a technical term which means the works by which God reveals himself and communicates with his creation. *Theologia* describes the inner life of God

'Almighty'

269   God has created all things, 'in heaven and on earth' (Ps 135,6), the Strength of Jacob, the Lord of armies, the strong, the valiant, for whom nothing is impossible, and to whom all things are subject 'because the whole world before him is like a speck that tips the scales' (Wis 11,22). Gen 1,1
Jn 1,3
Gen 49,24
Ps 24,8ff

270   Yet in his fatherhood, he shows at the same time his concern for us; 'I will be a father to you, and you shall be my sons and daughters' (2 Cor 6,18) and his great mercy which is ready to pardon our sins. There is no contradiction or arbitrariness in God, for his power and his wisdom are perfectly balanced by his justice and his mercy, and are as one in the simplicity of the Divine nature. Mt 6,32

Aquinas
ST 1,25,5
II–II,30,1

The apparent powerlessness of God

272   When we come in contact with evil and suffering, our faith in the Almighty power of God is put to the test. God seems to be absent, and powerless to prevent evil, just as Jesus seemed incapable to deal with the storm. But even as we see how the power of God was made manifest, so we see in the greater mystery of the Resurrection, how God conquers evil; for Christ, 'the power and wisdom of God', is that divine foolishness which in its weakness is Mk 4,37f

stronger than men. Nowhere can we see this better exemplified than in the Virgin Mary, who found that God looked on her lowliness because she believed that nothing was impossible for God. 'Besides, nothing serves so much to confirm our faith and hope, as to have it fixed in our hearts that with God all things are possible; for whatever we ought to believe, however great, however wonderful it may be, and however it may transcend the order and manner of things, easily and without hesitation obtains the assent of human reason, when once it has received the knowledge of the omnipotence of God.'

I Cor 1,24–25

Lk 1,48
Lk 1,37

RC 1,11,13

Creation

'Creator'

280 Creation is the foundation for God's plan of salvation which is fulfilled in Christ who inaugurates the new creation, as the new Adam. For this reason the Easter Vigil in the Byzantine liturgy always begins with the first reading from Genesis; and according to the Fathers the Creation account also began the instruction of the catechumens.

GCD 51
Gen 1,1

Egeria
pereg. 46

Creation in catechesis

282 The subject of creation is fundamental to human life, and even more important to a Christian because our final destiny is linked with the question of the beginning of all things.

NA 1

283 Modern discoveries concerning the date and size of the universe, the evolution of living things and the appearance of homo sapiens allow us to see the grandeur of God's creation in a new way. While we may dispute the exact manner of the emergence of man, and the cosmos itself, we ought to ask 'What is the meaning of both?' Are they the result of chance, or blind forces, or the creation of an Intelligence? How also do we explain evil? Some argue that the world and God are one reality, or one manifestation (pantheism); others that there are two eternal principles, good and evil, light and

Wis 7,17f

darkness in permanent conflict (dualism, Man-
icheism). According to certain thinkers the world
or matter, is evil and must be rejected (Gnosti-
cism); while others say that even if it is created by
God, it is abandoned to its own destiny (Deism); Pius XII
while others again take refuge in materialism and HG DS 3890
maintain that the world was a product of pre-
existent matter.

286 Man can by the aid of his own intelligence come to
an awareness of God as creator through the works Vatican I
of His hands, even if it is not a completely clear DS 3026
picture. But, since it is of such vital importance, Rom 1,20
God revealed to Israel bit by bit the mystery of his Heb 11,3
creation, because in choosing them, he created Acts 17,24
them and formed them, among all the peoples of Prov 8,22
the earth and the wonders of the heavens which Ps 115,15
owed their existence to Him. In the whole of Ps 124,8
Scripture, the first three chapters of Genesis hold Ps 134,3
pride of place. Is 43,1

Creation – a work of the Holy Trinity

290 'In the beginning, God created the heaven and the
earth'. He alone is the creator, and all that came to
be (= heaven and earth) owes its existence to Him.
But we need to add that 'in the beginning was the
Word ... all things were made through him and
without him was not anything made that was Col 1,16 –
made' (Jn 1,1–4). The Church also affirms that 17
the Holy Spirit is at work in creation, as Lord and Creed
giver of life, or, as in the *Veni, Creator Spiritus* Nic-Const
Hymn, the Creator Spirit. Creation is the Irenaeus
common work of the Holy Trinity: the Father AH 2,30,9
through His Word and His Wisdom. 4,20,1

The world has been created for the glory of God

293 S. Bonaventure explains that the world was
created not to increase the glory of God but to
show forth and share this glory. The purpose of
creation is that God should be all in all (I Cor
15,28), making us, his adoptive sons in Jesus Sent 2,1,
Christ, 'according to the purpose of his will to the 2,2,1
praise of his glorious grace which he freely Vatican I
bestowed on us in the Beloved.'(Eph 1,5–6). DS 3002

The mystery of creation

295 We believe that God did not create out of any need, but that he freely created out of nothing all that came to be: 'look at the heaven and the earth and see everything that is in them, and recognize that God did not make them out of things that existed. Thus also mankind comes into being' (2 Mac 7,28). Because God can create out of nothing, he can also create life in the soul of the sinner, dead in sin, as well as restore new physical life to the body in death, through resurrection.

Vatican I
DS 3022–5
DS 800

Ps 51,12
2 Cor 4,6
Rom 4,17

299 We are told that God found that what he created was *good*, proceeding from His own goodness, and reflecting also the wisdom of its creator in its structure which must never be considered as somehow evil. But at the same time God far surpasses His own creation, for 'in him, we live and move and have our being' (Acts 17,28). As S. Augustine says, 'He is loftier than my highest point and more inward than the innermost'. Yet at the same time he does not abandon his creation for a single instant.

Gen 1,4f
Wis 11,20
DS
286;455–
63;1333;
3002
Ps 8,2;
145,3
Conf
3,6,11
Mt 10,29

Divine providence : the realisation of God's plan

302 God's work of creation is not in its final state but yearning for that perfection to which it has been destined; and the means used we call divine providence. He remains totally in charge of all that happens : 'Many are the plans in the mind of man, but it is the purpose of the Lord that will be established' (Pro 19,21). For this reason we must have total confidence in Him.

Rom 8,22
Vatican I
DS 3003
Ps 115,3
Mt 6,31–33

Providence and secondary causes

306 God uses his creatures in the accomplishment of his plan, not as a sign of weakness, but as a manifestation of his goodness and power, to allow men especially to share in his work by their actions, prayers and sacrifices; 'for God is at work in you, both to will and to work for his good pleasure' (Phil 2,13).

Gen
1,26–28
Col 1,24
GS 36

Providence and the scandal of evil

309   God could have created a world in which evil
would not have existed, but chose to allow
contingency and *physical imperfection or natural
evil* which would be balanced by physical
perfection. He also chose to create free and
intelligent beings in the angels and humanity,
which allows for *moral evil* : sin, of which the
individual and not God is the cause. In his
providence God draws good even out of sin 'so
that in everything God works for good with those
who love him' (Rom 8,28). S. Thomas More
consoled his daughter before his martyrdom by
saying, 'Nothing can happen which was not willed
by God, because however bad it may appear to us,
because God willed it, it is best for us'.

Aquinas
ST 125,6
CG 3,71

Augustine
Lib 1,1,1
Enchir 11,3

Gen 45,8.50
Rom 5,20

'Heaven and earth'

327   The Fourth Lateran Council explains this by
saying that God 'from the very beginning of time
created out of nothing both orders of creatures,
the spiritual or angelic world and the corporeal or
visible universe'.

Lat IV
DS 800

Angels

328   The Church talks of spiritual beings, possessing
intelligence and will, who are immortal and
surpass in perfection all the visible universe. They
are called *angels* insofar as they are messengers
(*angeloi*) of God. They are more directly servants
of Christ, ministering to him, who announce his
birth, proclaim his glory to the shepherds, protect
his infancy, comfort him in his agony, proclaim
his resurrection and accompany him at the day of
final judgement.

Pius XII
HG
DS 3891

Mt 18,10
Aug
Ps 103,1,15
Col 1,16
Heb 1,6
Lk 1,11.26
Mt 1,20f
Lk 22,43
Mk 16,5–7
Mt 13,41

332   We notice that the angels are present in paradise,
protect Lot, save Hagar, forestall Abraham in his
sacrifice of Isaac, lead the people of Israel through
the desert, announce the birth of Samson and the

vocation of Gideon as well as come to the aid of Elijah.

335   In her liturgy the Church venerates the Archangels (29 September) and the guardian angels (2 October) with special feasts, invokes them at each Mass (*Sanctus, Sanctus, Sanctus* and *Supplices te rogamus . . .*) and in the funeral rite (*In Paradisum deducant te angeli . . .*)

The visible universe

337   The first chapter of Genesis presents the work of creation as taking place symbolically over six days, with God resting on the *Sabbath*. For this reason it is often known as the *priestly* account of creation. The passage teaches us that all things came to be through God's word and that everything has its own goodness and perfection, interrelated to the rest of creation, but leading up to man, who 'is worth more than many sparrows' (Mt 12,12).   Ps 8,6

Mankind

'Made in the image of God'

356   The human individual we call a *person* capable of knowing himself and possessing that knowledge in   GS 12
love, as well as of giving himself to other persons,   GS 24
because he is made in the image of his Creator,   GS 39
and alone is able to enter into communion with Him. God created everything for man, whose glory it is to love and serve Him. This mystery only becomes clear in the Word made flesh.   GS 22

Composed of body and soul

362   In the second account of creation, God 'formed man of dust from the earth, and breathed into his nostrils the breath of life; and man became a living   VS 48
being' (Gen 2,7). This breath of life is the *spiritual*   Mt 16,25−6
principle of man, his soul. It is *directly* and   2 Mac 6,30
immediately created by God, not by our parents,   1 Cor 6,19f
and is immortal. The human body, precisely   GS 14

because it is animated by the soul, will be raised up on the last day. [The Church has not pronounced definitely on man's evolution except to point out that this cannot apply to the soul and that any theory must take into account the inheritance of original sin by generation and not by imitation.]

Lat V
DS 1440
1 Thes 5,23
Paul VI
AAS (1966)
p. 654

'Man and woman he created them'

369   Man and Woman were created for each other, each reflecting the image of God so that they might complete each other, become one flesh in marriage, and so cooperate as parents in the work of creation.

Gen
2,19–20
Gen 2,24

In paradise

374   Our first parents, Adam and Eve, were created in a state of holiness and harmony with the rest of creation in which they were not meant to suffer or die, but to work in friendship with God.

Trent
DS 1511
LG 2
Gen 2,17.
Gen 3,16f

The Fall

Original sin – an essential truth of our faith

386   The mystery of sin can never be fully understood except in the light of the mystery of our faith which tells us that sin is not some genetic or psychological defect, or the consequence of social inadequacy but an abuse of the freedom with which we have been endowed by our creator. The full realisation of the sin of Adam can only be seen in the light of the Holy Spirit, sent by the risen Christ 'to convince the world of sin'.

2 Thes 2,7
1 Tim 3,16
Rom 5,20
VS 35

Jn,16,8

The fall of the angels

391   The voice of Satan is heard in paradise, 'that ancient serpent' who was created good but turned to evil, refusing to serve God and becoming a sinner from the beginning, the father of lies. His choice, and that of his companions in sin, was irrevocable, just as for man there is no repentance after death. But even if his malign influence makes

Rev 12,9
2 Pt 2,4
Lat IV
DS 800
1 Jn 3,8
Jn 8,44

itself felt in the life of Christ, it is precisely to destroy his work that the Son of God came, and Satan remains within the control of God's providence.

John Damas FO 2,4
Mt 4,1–11
I Jn 3,8

The first sin of man

396 Man, though free, cannot go against the structure of creation itself, or the restraints which liberty imposes symbolized by the 'fruit of the knowledge of good and evil'. But man wished to be like God, in control of his own destiny, and so suffered the consequences. Their eyes were opened indeed to a new world where disorder, disharmony and domination reigned, and the hostility of creation was matched by the enmity in humanity itself 'from the blood of Abel to the blood of Zechariah' (Lk 11,51). But the final bitter fruit was death.

Gen 2,17
Gen 3,5
Gen 3,7
Gen 3,11f
GS 13

Gen 3,19
Rom 5,12

The consequences of original sin for humanity

402 S. Paul teaches that 'by one man's disobedience many were made sinners' (Rom 5,19). This is not metaphor, but a tragic reality by which each of us inherit original sin, and need as infants that forgiveness which we obtain through Baptism.

Trent
DS 1512

404 Adam and Eve committed a personal sin. They were the first parents of our human nature and in sinning they 'changed it for the worse' and could not but transmit that state of sin to their descendants. We experience it most acutely in that wounding of our nature which inclines us to sin (= *concupiscence*) and creates a state of warfare within our mind and body. Baptism forgives the sin but cannot remove the wounds.

Trent
DS 1512

Rom 7,14f

406 S Augustine opposed *Pelagius* in the fifth century because he maintained that Adam's sin was merely bad example and that man could live morally without the assistance of grace. The 16th century reformers indentified original sin with concupiscence, and taught that mankind was totally corrupted and enslaved as a result of Adam's sin.

408   As a result we can talk of a certain evil influence
which affects human affairs: 'the whole world lies
in the power of the evil one' (1 Jn 5,19). However
man has been promised a new Adam who, by his
obedience unto death, will undo the disobedience
of the first Adam. For this reason Mary, the new
Eve, will be preserved from every stain of sin from
the first moment of her conception. The Church
says in the Easter Vigil 'O happy fault that won
for us so great a redeemer'.

GS 37
Rom
5,18–19
Phil 2,8

Pius IX
DS 2803
MR n.18

Chapter 2 Belief in Jesus Christ, Only Son of God

Jesus

430   'You shall call his name Jesus, for he will save his
people from their sins'(Mt 1,21). God does not
wish merely to save his people from slavery in
Egypt, but also from the greatest enslavement of
sin, because he alone can release mankind from
that bondage. The name *Jesus* means that God is
present to grant forgiveness and salvation, and
like that earlier saviour Joshua, lead his new
people to the kingdom of grace. In his resurrection
he shows the victory he wins over sin and death, to
merit a 'name that is above all other names' (Phil
2, 9–10) which is invoked in the Church as the
source of all grace and the heart of all prayer,
frequently on the lips of dying Christians.

DT 5,6
Mk 2,7

Jos 1,2

Jn 12,28
Acts 16,16f
Mk 16,17
Jn 15,16

Christ

436   The word *Christ* is the Greek translation of the
Hebrew word *Messiah*, which means *anointed*:
anointed by the Lord to be king, priest and
prophet. He would fulfil the promises given to
Israel and who God anointed with the Holy Spirit
and with power so that he might be revealed to his
people as son of David. But not as King except on
the Cross, for he did not wish any political power,
but only the role of Suffering Servant whose
kingdom was not of this world.

Zch 4,14
Is 61,1
Lk 4,16–21
Jn 10,36
Mt 1,16
Acts 10,38
Jn 18,37
Jn 6,15
Mt 20,28

Only Son of God

441 The title *son of God* was given to angels, the   Job 1,6
Chosen People and their kings, and expresses that   Ex 4,22
protective concern of God even in the case of the   Ps 82,6
Messiah. Yet it required a special revelation to   Ps 2,7
allow Peter to recognise Christ as 'the Son of the
living God' (Mt 16,16) and to reveal it to Paul.   Acts 9,20
The evangelists begin the public ministry of Christ
with the declaration at his baptism by the Father
as he was overshadowed by the Spirit in the form
of a dove that he is the beloved Son in whom the
Father is well pleased. He affirmed that he was   Mt 3,17
consecrated and sent into the world by the Father,   cf 17,5
and indeed was one with him; as he admitted   Jn 10,36
before the Sanhedrin and as was proved by his   Jn 10,30
resurrection, 'Son of God by his power' (Rom   Lk 2,70
1,4).   Jn 1,14

Lord

446 *Lord* is the normal rendering of YHWH. Jesus
rarely uses it of himself but it is seen as an
affirmation of the honour due to him because in
his resurrection he has been exalted above every
name in creation. The Church waits for his final   Phil 2,9f
triumph, saying, 'Come, Lord Jesus'(Rev 22,20)   GS 10

Jesus Christ was conceived by the Holy Spirit and born of the Virgin Mary

Why did the Word become incarnate?

456 The great mystery of our religion is that 'He was   I Jn 4,2
manifested in the flesh' (I Tim 3,16). He became   Heb 10,5f
man for us and for our salvation, so as to take   I Jn 3,5
away our sins, and to make visible the love of God   I Jn 4,9
and invite us to follow him and become sharers in   Mt 11,29
the divine nature.   2 Pt 1,4

True God and true man

464 Christianity has always insisted that the Son of   I Jn 4,2
God has come in the flesh. The Church had to   DS 126
defend this position against *Arius* in the 4th   DS 130
century, who said that 'before the Son was

begotten, he was not'. Instead Nicea professed that The Lord Jesus Christ is consubstantial (*homoousios*) with the Father. The Council of Ephesus in 431 maintained against the *Nestorians* that 'the Word united to himself in his own person, a body animated by a rational soul ... and became man' – one divine person of whom Mary is the Mother so that she can be called Mother of God (Theotokos). The Monophysites went further and said that Christ's human nature had been assumed by the Person of the Word, and were condemned by the Council of Chalcedon (451). The Church therefore confesses that Jesus is true God and true man, 'remaining what he was, and assuming what he was not' as the *Benedictus* antiphon says on the first of January in the Roman Liturgy.

DS 250
DS 251

DS 301–2

The soul and human consciousness of Christ

471   The Son of God, in assuming human nature, possessed a human soul with all that it implies: 'he increased in wisdom and in stature and in grace' (Lk 2,52). His human knowledge was limited and experimental, but at the same time he possessed that deep knowledge of humanity because he was the Word of God. There was no opposition in Christ, but rather that total obedience, even to death on the Cross, for which reason the Church sees in the devotion to the Sacred Heart the human love of the divine redeemer 'who loved me and gave himself for me' (Gal 2,20).

DS 149
Mk 6,38
4,27;
Jn 11,34.
Jn 2,25
Mk, 14,36
DS 556–9
Pius XII
Haur Aquas
DS 3924

Conceived by the power of the Holy Spirit

484   The answer to Mary's question : 'How shall this be?' was 'The Holy Spirit will come upon you, and the power of the Most High will overshadow you' (Lk 1,35). 'The Lord and giver of life, sanctifies her womb so that the Son of God may take flesh within her.

Born of the virgin Mary

487   Eve was promised that one of her descendants would crush the head of the serpent, reversing by

LG 55–6
Gen 3,15.2

obedience the disobedience of the first mother of all the living. In the fulness of time God 'sent his angel to a virgin betrothed to a man named Joseph of the house of David and the virgin's name was Mary' (Lk 1,26−27). He made her 'full of grace' (Lk 1,28) in view of the sinless Son of God who would be her son; and we believe her to be immaculate from the moment of her conception according to the dogma proclaimed by Pius IX in 1854.

Eph 1,3

DS 2803
LG 56

The virginity of Mary

496 The Church holds that Jesus was conceived in the womb of Mary 'not with human seed but of the Holy Spirit', so fulfilling the prophecy of Isaiah 'a virgin shall conceive and bear a son and shall call him Immanuel' (Is 7,14). She is, and remains forever a virgin, *Aeiparthenos*, while being the Mother of God and of all those who are brethren in her Son.
[James and Joseph named in the Gospel as the 'brothers of Jesus' (Mt 13,55) are in fact sons of 'the other Mary', disciple of Christ, who were related to him as 'his brethren' cf. Gen 13,8; 14,16; 29,15.]

Lat I
DS 503
Mt 1,20

LG 52
LG 63
Rom 8,29
Heb 2,11
LG 63−4

501 Mary is virgin and mother in the same way that the Church remains pure in faith, while bringing forth new children for God in baptism.

LG 63−4

The mysteries of Christ's life

514 The evangelists, as they meditated on the life of Christ, in whom the whole fullness of deity dwelt bodily, saw his humanity as a 'sacrament' of the salvation he came to bring : a revelation and the mystery of our redemption. We are called to live those mysteries in our own life.

Col 2,9
Jn 14,9
Mt 8,17
GS 22

The birth and hidden life

522 Christ the mediator of a new covenant is foretold in various ways by the prophecies, but announced in the last days by John the Baptist, the last and greatest prophet who greeted him even in the womb

Heb 9,15
Lk 1,76
Lk 7,28
Lk 1,41

and gives his life in martyrdom for him. The Church celebrates such preparation at each Advent, looking forward also to that second coming of Christ at the end of time. Jesus was born in a stable at Bethlehem 'because there was no room for them in the inn' (Lk 2,7), showing us that we need to become as children and allow Christ to be reborn in us. By his *circumcision* he is made a subject of the law and a member of Abraham's race. The *Epiphany* is that *manifestation* to the gentiles by means of the star of David, that Jesus will be the king of all nations, and that 'the gentiles are called to become part of the family of the patriarchs'. The *Presentation in the Temple* shows him as the first born of the Lord, and the glory of Israel; the *flight into Egypt* is a sign of the opposition to him, and also prophesies that Jesus will bring about that new and final Exodus. *The Finding of the child Jesus in the Temple* allows us to see that obedience to the Father's will while remaining subject to Mary and Joseph.

Mk 6,17 – 29
Rev 22,17

Mt 18,3
Gal 4,19
Gal 4,4
Num 24,17

Leo I
Serm 23
Ex 13,12 – 13
Lk 2,32

Hos 11,1
Mt 2,15
Lk 2,51

The mysteries of the public life of Jesus

535 The *Baptism* of Jesus is his *Epiphany* as Messiah and beloved Son of God, but in joining with the sinners to be baptized, Jesus takes on his role as suffering servant 'being numbered with the transgressors' (Is 53,12), looking forward to the 'baptism' of his death when as lamb of God he would take away the sins of the world and see heaven once again thrown open which Adam's sin had closed.

Mt 3,13f

Lk 12,50
Jn 1,29
Mt 3,16

538 In his *temptation in the desert*, Jesus unlike the sons of Israel who for forty years put God to the test, remains faithful and overcomes the tempter, winning for us the victory. We celebrate this every *Lent*.

Ps 95,9
Mk 3,27
Heb 4,15

541 The *kingdom of God* which is for all mankind, belongs especially to the poor and the sinners who are invited to enter by means of *parables* and 'wonders and signs which God did through him' (Acts 2,22). The healing of the hungry and the

LG 5

sick, as well as the casting out of devils, is the sign   Jn 8,34f
of the victory of Christ over sin and the prince of   Jn 12,31
this world. He makes this kingdom rest on the
foundations of his twelve apostles, of whom   Lk 22,29f
Simon Peter is made the rock on which, as the
living stone, he will build his Church. He also
gives him the keys and makes him the chief pastor
of that flock of which He is the Good Shepherd,
conferring on the apostles in that authority of
binding and loosing which pertains to the teaching
of doctrine in the Church.   Mt 18,18

554   The *Transfiguration*, which follows Peter's confession of faith looks forward to the glory which   Lk 24,26
Christ enters by his resurrection, and our own,   Aquinas
when he will 'transfigure our lowly bodies and   ST 3,45,4
make them like his own' (Phil 3,21). But as Moses
and Elijah talked about his passion, so we are
reminded that 'through many tribulations we
must enter the Kingdom of God' (Acts 14,22).

557   *Jesus enters Jerusalem* as son of David coming to
claim his inheritance, yet humble, riding on a   Lk 1,32
donkey. The Church celebrates this solemnly on   Mt 21,38
Palm Sunday, and with the *Sanctus* begins the   Zch 9,9
Eucharistic Prayer at Mass.   Ps 118,26

'He suffered under Pontius Pilate, was crucified, died and was buried'

574   *Jesus and Israel*

Jesus and the Law: Jesus came to fulfil the law   Mt 5,17
down to the last dot, which the Jews themselves   Jas 2,1
found impossible, burdened as it was with human
traditions, which made void the commandments.
Jesus argued that the Law is written in the heart,   Mk 7,8
and gave that deep interpretation which went to   Mk 7,13
the root of the divine covenant between God and   Jer 31,
Israel.   Mt 5,33

583   *Jesus and the Temple*: Jesus' life is marked by   Jn 5,1.
pilgrimages to the Temple, the place dedicated to   14;7,1f
his Father, for which he showed his reverence
when he drove out the merchants. The destruction
of the Temple would only be replaced by that   Mt 21,1
worship of His own Presence.   Mt 12,6

597   *The Jews and the death of Jesus*

From the cross, Jesus pardoned those who put
him to death, of whom Peter maintained that they
had acted 'out of ignorance' (Acts 3,17) from
which it follows that 'neither all Jews indis-
criminately at that time, nor Jews today can be
charged with this crime'. All sinners are   NA 4
responsible for the suffering and death of Christ,   Heb 6,6
especially those baptized in his death.   RC 1,5,11

The crucifixion of Jesus

599   The death of Jesus for our sins was 'according to
the Scriptures' (I Cor 15,3) says St Paul, and   Acts 4,28
according to the predestined plan of God who sent   I Pt 1,18f
his Son to take on our sins, so that we might be   2 Cor 5,21
reconciled through his death and *all* might find   Rom 8,32
forgiveness. Jesus willingly surrenders his life, as   Rom 5,10
the Lamb, which was the symbol of Israel's   DS 624
redemption on that first Passover, giving his life   Ex 12,3f
as a ransom for many, out of supreme love.   Mk 10,45

610   The night on which he was betrayed, he expressed   Lk 22,19
that love in instituting the Eucharist, in his body   Mt 26,28
given for us and his blood *shed* for all for the   I Cor 11,25
forgiveness of sins. The impact of those sins was
experienced by Jesus in his agony and sweat of
blood in Gethsemane, and consummated in his   Lk 22,44
sacrifice on the Cross, the perfect expiation for the   Trent
sins of the world. We are called to take up our   DS 1529
cross and follow him, because he has left us an   Mt 16,24
example that we should follow in his steps.   I Pt 2,21

The burial of Jesus

624   Jesus truly suffered the separation of his soul
from his body, but 'he is the first and last, and the
living one; I died, and behold I am alive for
evermore' (Rev 1,18). With him we are called to
enter into his death, so that we might rise to
newness of life in baptism.   Rom 6,4

'He descended to the dead. On the third day he rose again.'

632   The completion of the work of the Messiah is that
of preaching the Gospel 'to the spirits in prison'

(I Pt 3,19) who, like Lazarus 'in the bosom of Abraham' waited to be delivered from death by the author of life 'who holds the key of death and Hades' (Rev 1,18).

638 *The resurrection of Christ* on the third day is an historical fact established by the empty tomb found in such a way as to convince the witnesses that Christ had truly risen, and confirmed by his appearances first to the women and then to many witnesses, including 500 on one occasion. The fact that many continued to doubt further reinforces the objective reality of the Risen Christ: 'See my hands and my feet, that it is I myself; handle me and see; for a spirit has not flesh and bones as you see I have' (Lk 24,39). Yet Christ was raised in glory, the first fruits of all who fall asleep, death having no more dominion over him, and able to move through time and space in a new way.

Lk 24,9f
1 Cor 15,6

648 We can say that Christ was raised by the power of the Father through the work of the Holy Spirit, yet also we can talk of the Son of God laying down his life so as to take it up again. It is a work of the whole Trinity so that 'we might live no longer for ourselves but for Him who for (our) sake died and was raised' (2 Cor 5,15).

Acts 2,2
Rom 1,3−4

Jn 10,18

'He ascended into heaven, and is seated at the right hand of the Father'

659 When Jesus appeared to Mary Magdalen he said that he had not yet ascended to his Father; having come down from heaven he would return to that place in heaven where he is given 'dominion and glory and kingdom, that all peoples, nations and languages should serve him' (Dan 7,14) which shall never end.

Jn 20,17
Jn 3,13

'He will come again to judge the living and the dead'

668 At his ascension, Christ said to his apostles 'All authority on heaven and on earth has been given to me' (Mt 28,18). He is Lord of all creation, of the living and the dead, as well as Head of the Church, which is his Body, through the redemption which he won for her.

Eph 1,20f
Rom 14,9
Eph 1,22
Eph 4,11f

671   However the ascension did not mark the coming
       of the kingdom in glory, but the beginning of the   Acts 1,6–7
       last days during this time we must watch out   Rev 22,20
       because this is also the time of trial. Before the end   1 Jn 2,18
       we will see the final persecution and the coming of   1 Cor 7,26
       Anti-Christ. It is only after that persecution that   2 Thes 2,4f
       Israel will be welcomed into the salvation pre-   Rom 11,12
       pared for them, and God will be all in all.   1 Cor 15,28

676   The need to avoid false messiahs proclaiming the
       final days was pointed out by Christ (Mt 24,24)
       and S. Paul (I Thes 5,1) but *Millenarians* still
       continue to collect followers, frequently with
       tragic results when hopes are not realised.

678   The Father has given all power of judgement to   Jn 5,22
       the Son, who at the last day will bring to light the   Lk 12,1–3
       secret thoughts of all. Then those who have   Rom 2,16
       wilfully rejected the grace of God and his love and   Mt 11,20f
       turned away from their neighbour will be found   Mt 25,45
       worthy of the eternal punishment which they have   Jn 3,18
       chosen by their actions.   Heb 6,4–6

Chapter 3 Belief in the Holy Spirit

683   When the Father sends into our hearts the Spirit of   Gal 4,6
       his Son, we know that in Christ we see our God
       made visible, but it is through the Holy Spirit that
       He is revealed to us. He is anointed for his mission
       by the Spirit who will later glorify Him, 'for he
       will take what is mine and declare it to you' (Jn
       16,14).   Jn 17,22

The names and symbols of the Holy Spirit

691   The term *Spirit* is a translation of the Hebrew   Jn 3,5–8
       Ruah meaning breath, or wind. Jesus refers to the   I Jn 2,1
       sending of *another* Advocate (Paraclete) who will   Jn 16,13
       also be the Spirit of Truth, as He bears witness to
       the truth.
       The Spirit is also seen as *living water*, welling up to   Jn 4,14
       eternal life and *unction*, for Jesus becomes the   Acts 2,3
       Christ through the Holy Spirit who anoints Him.
       The Holy Spirit appears at Pentecost in the form
       of tongues of *fire* transforming the apostles, as

earlier he had taken hold of the prophets. The
appearances of God in the Old Testament were frequently accompanied by the *cloud* (shekinah) and
the *light*, signs of His glory which were seen by the
apostles on the Mount of Transfiguration. The Holy
Spirit is also identified with the *seal* that marks the
anointing that theologians term the *character* of the
sacraments of baptism, confirmation and Holy
Orders, which cannot be repeated. The Holy Spirit
under the form of a *dove* descended on Jesus at his
baptism, and was for Noah the sign of the new
creation after the flood. The imparting of the Holy
Spirit by *epiclesis* is traditionally accompanied by
an imposition of hands

Sir 48,1
Ex 24,15f
Ex 40,36f
Lk 9,28f

The Spirit and the Word of God

702 The work of creation comes about by the Word
and the Spirit for 'by his word the heavens were
made, by the breath of his mouth all the stars'
(Ps. 33,6).

Ps 104,30

705 It is the Holy Spirit that accomplishes the promise
made to Abraham, in his descendant, who will be
Christ and those whom he gathers together. He is
manifested in the desert by means of the cloud,
through whom the Word of God is revealed. He
later speaks through the prophets of the Messiah
who will be filled with the gifts of the Spirit 'to
bring the Gospel to the poor, to bind up the
broken-hearted, to proclaim release to the
captives and recovering of sight to the blind, to set
the prisoners free and to proclaim a year of grace
from the Lord' (Is 61,1−2; Lk 4,18−19). The
Holy Spirit will create in mankind a new heart,
preparing those who look for the consolation of
Israel to receive him in the fullness of time. John
the Baptist 'who is filled with the Holy Spirit even
from his mother's womb (Lk 1,15), went before
the Lord to prepare his path and to bear witness
that he had seen the Spirit descend upon him.

Eph 3,14

Is 11,1−2

Lk 1,17
Lk 2,25
Jn 1,33−36

Mary, full of grace

721 Tradition calls Mary, *Seat of Wisdom* and applies
to her many of the texts from the Wisdom

literature, because she is the masterpiece of God's creation, filled with grace by the Holy Spirit so that she can be a worthy dwelling-place for the only Son of God. She is that most humble and most pure virgin daughter of Sion who becomes the new Eve, mother of all who live.

Jesus, and the Holy Spirit

727   Jesus does not talk plainly about the Holy Spirit   Jn 3,5-8
before his death and resurrection. He refers to the   Jn 4,10f
Spirit in his conversation with Nicodemus and the   Jn 6,63
Samaritan woman, when he talks to the crowds
after the feeding of the five thousand, and at the
feast of Tabernacles. He only talks openly to his
disciples when it is a question of the witness they   Jn 7,37-39
are to bear to Christ and the manner in which they   Mt 10,19f
are to pray to the Father.   Lk 11,13

729   When the hour comes when he will be glorified,
Jesus promises that the Spirit, sent by the Father,
will bring honour to him because he will take from
what is his and declare it to them, leading them
into all truth 'as He convinces the world of sin, of   Jn 16,15
justice and of judgement.'   Jn 16,8

The Spirit in the Church

737   Jesus pours out the Spirit on his apostles, giving
them the mission that had been confided to him by
the Father, which would include the work of   Jn 20,21
drawing mankind into communion with the   Rom 8,23
Trinity. It is through the Spirit that we receive the   Gal 5,22-3
first fruits of our inheritance: which comes to us
from our incorporation into Christ through
baptism. These will be discussed later under the
section dealing with theological virtues (n.1830).
It is the Holy Spirit that helps us in our weakness,
'for we do not know how to pray as we ought, but
the Spirit himself intercedes for us with sighs too
deep for words, for no one comprehends the   Rom 8,26
thoughts of God except the Spirit' who searches   1 Cor 2,11
everything, even the depths of God.   Gal 4,6

§1 Belief in the holy Catholic Church

748 'Since we have shown that the Holy Spirit is the
source and giver of all holiness, we now profess
our belief that the Church has been endowed by   RC 1,10,1
him with sanctity'   LG 1

The names and symbols of the Church

751 The word *ekklèsia* taken from the Greek, meaning
convocation, is used in connection with the
assembly of the people of Israel during their time
in the wilderness. The use of the same term by the
Church recognises that this is the assembly of the   1 Cor 11,18
new Israel, who at the same time are a liturgical   1 Cor 1,2
community, a local body and a universal Church.   Gal 1,13

753 The Church is therefore the *People of God*, and   Eph 1,22
the Body of which Christ is the Head. But it can   Jn 10,1–10
also be described in terms of a *flock*, a field in   I Cor 3,9
which grows the *olive tree* and *the vine*; it is also   Mt 21,33f
the building, the family, and above all the temple,   I Tim 3,15
built upon the corner stone which is Christ, and   Eph 2,
our heavenly Jerusalem, the spouse of the   19–22
immaculate Lamb.   1 Pt 2,5
    Gal 4,26
    Rev 21,2.9

The Church in God's plan

759 God wished to call mankind to share his divine life
through his Son, and those who believe in his Son
are called to form his holy Church: 'The world
was created for the Church' says Pastor Hermas,   LG 1
so integral is it to God's plan.   Vis 2,4,1

760 It was made doubly necessary with the advent of
sin, to reassemble the scattered people of the
world, divided and at enmity. God made   Gen 12,2
Abraham the father of a great people, and Israel   Is 2,2–5
the sign for that future ingathering of the nations.   Mic 4,1–4

763 Jesus chose the Twelve to represent the twelve   Mt 19,28
tribes of Israel, who would also be the foundation   Lk 22,30
stones of the new Jerusalem. It was born from the   Rev 21,
side of Christ sleeping on the Cross, from that blood   12–14

and water poured out from Him. The Holy Spirit
prompts within the Church those charisms which
lead to holiness and fraternal love while order-
ing the structure hierarchically. It will only be   SC 5
made perfect when its final pilgrimage is over and   LG 4
Christ comes again to deliver the kingdom to his   1 Cor 15,
Father.   24

The Church, a mystery of the union of God and mankind

772   S. Paul talks of a 'great mystery ... in reference
to Christ and the Church' (Eph 5,32). In fact the   LG 9
Church is the *sacrament* of the profound union
between mankind and God and of His love; as
well as looking forward to that universal
redemption from every nation and race and   Rev 7,9
people when there will be only one Body, and one   AG 7
temple of the Living God.
[*mystérion* can be translated from Greek into the
Latin *mysterium* meaning the hidden reality of
our salvation, and *sacramentum* its visible sign.]

The Church — People of God, Body of Christ, Temple of the Holy Spirit

782   *The People of God* share in Christ's function as   LG 10
priest, prophet and king. By baptism they are
consecrated, by their supernatural appreciation of
the faith and their growth in the knowledge and
love of the truths of their religion. They share in   LG 12
the prophetic role of Christ, and in their service of   CL 9
Him who came to serve and not to be served, they   Mt 20,28
reign with him.   LG 36

787   *The Body of Christ* is that mysterious and deep   LG 7
communion which exists between his body and our   Rom 12,4
own, which is not simply an association with him   Jn 15, 4–
but a sharing in his very life. This does not abolish   Gal 4,19
our diversity for he lives in us as the vine in the   Eph 4,11
branches, uniting us to his Passion and making us   Aquinas
grow up in all things into him, our head.   ST 3,48,2

The spouse of Christ

796   The Lord described himself as the Bride, and S.
Paul presents the Church and each faithful

member as betrothed to Christ – as a pure bride
to her one husband. She is that immaculate bride
of the pure lamb whom Christ loved and for   Mk 2,19
whom he delivered himself so as to sanctify her,   2 Cor 11,2
nourishing and cherishing her so that she might be   Rev 22,17
holy and without blemish.   Eph 5,25f

The temple of the Holy Spirit

797   The Holy Spirit is that 'principal of every living   Pius XII
and truly supernatural act in all parts of the   Mys Corp
Body'. By the word of God the Church is built up;   DS 3808
by baptism the Body is formed; by the sacraments   Acts 20,32
growth and healing are given to the members and   I Cor 12,13
by the gifts and virtues the whole Body is ordered   LG 12
and governed for the common good.   1 Cor 12,7

The Church is one, holy, catholic and apostolic

811   Vatican I reminds us that 'the Church itself,
because of its holiness, its catholic unity and its
invincible constancy, is a great and perpetual
motive of credibility and an irrefutable proof of   DS 3013
its own divine mission'. The four marks are
inseparable from the structure of the Church:
'Hence it is that the Church that really is catholic,
must at the same time be marked out by the
prerogatives of unity, holiness and apostolic
succession.'   DS 2888

The Church is one

813   The Church's unity stems from the unity of the   UR 2
Trinity itself, but also because it has Christ alone
as its founder, 'for no other foundation can any
one lay than that which is laid, which is Jesus
Christ' (I Cor 3,11). It has also one principle of   GS 78
unity, the Holy Spirit who pervades and rules the
whole Church, eager to maintain that legitimate
diversity of gifts and devotions, as well as rites and
traditions in the body of peace.   Eph 4,3

815   The interior bond of unity is that charity 'which
binds everything together in perfect harmony',
(Col 3,14), but the external ties are the profession
of one faith, received from the apostles; the

common celebration of a single worship, especially with reference to the sacraments, and apostolic succession handed on by the sacrament of Orders.

817   S. Paul lamented that there were dissensions among the Christians of Corinth and asked 'Is Christ divided?' (I Cor 1,13). Such divisions due to sin whether of heresy, apostasy or schism are unfortunately stili with us, but we must   CIC 751
distinguish between committing the sin and being born into a community that has separated from the Church, such a distinction is especially important in the case of those who through baptism are our brethren in Christ. Through a reverence for the word of God, a life of grace and faith, hope and the practice of charity they draw life from the Church, and are led towards that unity for which Christ prayed at the hour of his passion 'that they may all be one; even as we are one, I in them and thou in me, that they may become perfectly one, so that the world may know that thou hast sent me' (Jn 17,21). It is to the   UR 1
Church of which Peter is the head, that Christ gave the abundant riches of the new covenant and   UR 3
all who are already Christians find full communion in the Catholic Church. For this to take place, there must be a greater fidelity in the Church to her vocation which involves conversion   UR 6
of heart, prayer together as well as collaboration   UR 7
in the social field and mutual understanding which   UR 12
extends to matters of theology. We trust in   UR 9
Christ's prayer, which surpasses human efforts,   UR 10
that we may reach that day when there can be one   UR 24
Church.   UR 4

The Church is holy

823   As Christ, the Son of God is called in the *Gloria*, *solus Sanctus*, the Church is the holy People of   LG 12
God and the members also 'saints'. Yet the   Acts 9,13
Church also *sanctifies*: in her we acquire holiness   1 Cor 6,1
being called to become perfect even as our heavenly Father is perfect, with that love which has been given to us by him who first loved us   Mt 5,48
while we were still sinners. The darnel of sin is   LG 42

mixed with the good grain of God's word until the
end of time, but the Church embraces sinners,
calling them to repentance and to that holiness
which is the final goal.

1 Jn 4,10
Mt 13,24f
SPF 19
LG 8

828 The Saints who have been *canonised* for their
heroic practice of virtue and their fidelity to divine
grace are both our intercessors and our model, as
is our blessed Lady who in her holiness mirrors
that perfection which is the Church's own.

LG 65

The Church is catholic

830 The Church is catholic both because it possesses
the totality of the means of salvation and also
because it is sent to the whole of humanity. Christ
is present in each community, when the people are
gathered together to hear the word of God and
celebrate the holy Eucharist, realising his Church,
one, holy, catholic and apostolic. The dioceses (or
eparchies) as *particular Churches*, whose bishops
share in apostolic succession, are images of the
whole Catholic Church by their communion with
the Church of Rome which presides over all in
charity.

AG 6

LG 26

CIC 368–
369
Ign Ant
Rom 1,1

835 The universal Church is not the sum of the
particular Churches, nor a federation presided
over by a chairman. Episcopal conferences
drawing together various dioceses on a territorial
basis are administrative groupings to facilitate
inter-diocesan exchanges. Their decisions, taken
by a two-thirds majority, are subject to review by
the Apostolic See.

CIC 454

Who belongs to the Church?

836 Firstly, those who accept all the means of
salvation and are in full communion with the
hierarchical structure of the Church, accepting
her teaching in faith and morals. Those who have
reservations on any of those items may be said to
be in the Church in body, but not in mind and
heart.

LG 14

838 Secondly, those who accept the means of salvation, but do not recognise the authority of the Roman Pontiff. This applies to the *Orthodox Churches* who share a very deep communion with the Catholic Church.
Thirdly those who are united with us in baptism but do not accept the other sacraments, nor the authority of the Pope, whom we call separated Christian brethren.

The Church and non-christians

839 Among those who are not Christian who hold pride of place are the Jewish people, the first to hear the word of God, 'adopted as God's sons, to whom belong the glory, the covenants, the giving of the law, the worship and the promises; of whom are the patriarchs, and of their race, according to the flesh, is the Christ ... (for) God never takes back his gifts or revokes his choice (Rom 9,4–5;11,29). The followers of *Islam* worship one God and accept the faith of Abraham. But the plan of salvation also extends to those who seek the unknown God in shadows and images, but given original sin, find the search hard and painful. It is because of this that the Church has a duty to evangelise the whole of humanity so that each may find in the Church that ark of salvation, which is guided by the breath of the Holy Spirit, sailing under the sign of our Lord's cross.

LG 16

LG 14
AG 7

Ambrose
virg 18,118

The Church is apostolic

857 The Church is apostolic because it is built on the foundation of the apostles, on their faith and their witness, which it maintains in fidelity to them through the apostolic succession of bishops and priests.

The bishops, successors of the apostles

Jn 20,21

861 Christ chose the apostles to continue his own mission and gave them the power to be his ministers, and to rule over the Church after he had ascended to his Father, until the end of time. The

LG 20

Church therefore teaches that the bishops succeed
the apostles by divine institution as pastors of the
Church, in such a way that who ever listens to
them, hears Christ, and who ever rejects them,
rejects Christ and the One who sent him. The   LG 20
successor of the chief of the apostles is the Pope,
the bishop of Rome, with whom all bishops have
that loyal communion. He is the perpetual and·
visible source and foundation of that unity which
binds together both the bishops and all the faithful   LG 23
of the Church, because he is that rock on which
Jesus built his Church, to whom alone he gave the
keys, and whom he made shepherd of his whole
flock. For this reason the Pope is said to possess
full, supreme and universal power which he can
freely exercise in any part of the Church of which
he is *the Bishop*, to use the title with which he signs   LG 22
the documents of a General Council. He is also
head of the episcopal *College*, which with him
exercises supreme plenary power over the Church   CIC 336–7
(especially, in a General Council) but only with his   LG 22
confirmation.   CIC 336

886   The bishops are each the source and foundation of   LG 23
unity for their particular dioceses, exercising their   CD 3
pastoral authority over that portion of the People
of God confided to them, assisted by priest and
deacons. But as members of the episcopal college
they have that concern for all the Churches of   Gal 2,10
which S. Paul speaks. This means that they govern
well their own Church, contribute to the well-
being of the universal Church and in practical
ways assist the poor, those who are persecuted for
the faith and those engaged as Christian mission-
aries, taking the Gospel to the ends of the earth.

880   Christ intending that the faith should be handed
on faithfully by the apostles and their successors
without any mixture of error, made them sharers
in his own infallibility, so that the People of God
by their supernatural grasp of the faith may,
under guidance of the teaching authority of the
bishops (*Magisterium*), reflect Christ, the Truth.

891   This infallibility applies to the Roman Pontiff   Lk 22,31
when as shepherd and teacher of all the faithful,

with the task of confirming his brothers in the faith, he proclaims by virtue of his supreme apostolic authority a point of doctrine concerning faith or morals to be held by the universal church. Such a guarantee of freedom from error extends to the college of bishops teaching in communion with the successor of Peter especially when gathered in a General Council, but also when they exercise their ordinary teaching authority (Magisterium) proposing a valid development in the understanding of the Church's deposit concerning faith or morals: in union with the successor of Peter. Their authority in their dioceses is in fact asserted, strengthened and vindicated by that universal and supreme authority of the Pope, the universal pastor of the Church.

Vatican I
DS 3074

LG 25
Vatican I
DS 3061

The lay faithful

898 The lay people of the Church, by virtue of their baptism and confirmation, are called to the apostolate of engaging in temporal affairs and directing them to the service of God, and to sharing in the redemptive work of Christ. They have the right either individually or as groups to act as the leaven in secular society, which is their own special vocation.

CIC 225

LG 31
CL 15

901 a) They share in Christ's priestly office by gathering up all their activities and making them into a spiritual sacrifice acceptable to God. Married people exercise this spiritual ministry when they bring up their children in the knowledge and love of God; the sick by offering their illnesses; those who are assailed by temptations, by offering their struggles.

2 Pt 2,5

CIC 835

904 b) They share in the prophetic office of Christ by bearing witness to the message of the Gospel, making a defence of the hope that is in them through religious instruction, and all the communications media now available for spreading the word of God.

Aquinas
ST 3,71,4

1 Pt 3,15
CIC 212

908 c) They share in Christ's royal office by that   VS 13
      conquest of themselves in body and soul which
      enables them to be truly free so as to serve
      Christ and influence the moral climate by their
      practice of virtue. They are at the same time,   EN 73
      through their own unique individual gifts, the
      witness and the living instrument of the
      mission of the Church in the environment in
      which they live and work.   LG 33

The consecrated life

915 Everyone is called to practise chastity, poverty
      and obedience if they wish to belong to the
      kingdom of God, but those who profess the
      counsels in a stable way of life belong to the   LG 42–3
      religious state. This takes various forms under the PC I
      inspiration of the Holy Spirit.   CIC 573

The eremitical life

920 Consists in a silent and solitary consecration of
      prayer and penance in praise of God and for the
      salvation of the world and is a special imitation of
      Christ in the desert. That total dedication to God
      and for God is the response of one who wishes to
      imitate Christ by separation from the world, in its
      most acute form.   CIC 603

Consecrated virginity

922 'For the sake of the kingdom of heaven' (Mt
      19,12) either living in the world or in community,   1 Cor 7,
      dedicated to prayer, penance and charitable works   34–36
      is a special state of service in the Church. It is an CIC 604
      expressive sign of the love of the Church for   MR
      Christ and recalls us to that first innocence which Pref 68
      anticipates the life of the world to come.   Mt 22,30

The religious life

925 Began with the Egyptian monks of the first   UR 15
      centuries of Christianity and is marked out by the CIC 607
      way in which its members celebrate the liturgy,
      live the common life and bear witness to the

practical love of God. They co-operate with the local bishop in his pastoral office, whether they are directly under the jurisdiction of the Holy See or not. They include the great monastic orders and missionary congregations.   CIC 591

930 Members of *societies of apostolic life* are dedicated to a life of perfection and charity, according to their own constitutions but without vows.   PC 1

Secular institutes

928 Enable people to live a secular life while being the leaven in the world, through imbuing all things with the spirit of the Gospel. *Covenant Communities* of the Charismatic Renewal would largely fall under this category.   PC 11   CIC 713

Personal prelatures

Personal prelatures are set up by the Holy See, under a prelate who is the Ordinary with jurisdiction over the secular clergy of the prelature and the lay people associated with it, for certain pastoral or missionary activities as laid down in their rules.   PO 10   AG 20   CIC 294–7

'Among the clergy and the laity are Christian faithful who are consecrated to God in their own special manner and serve the saving mission of the Church through the evangelical counsels.' (CIC 207)

§2 The Communion of Saints

946 The term 'communion of saints' means both communion with holy things (*sancta*) and communion between holy people (*sancti*). The faithful (*sancti*) are nourished with the Body and Blood of Christ (*sancta*) so that they can increase in Communion (*koinônia*) with the Holy Spirit.

A communion of spiritual gifts (sancta)

949 The Acts of the Apostles tell us that the disciples 'devoted themselves to the apostles' teaching and fellowship, to the breaking of bread and the prayers' (Acts 2,42).

There is a communion in the faith received from the apostles, joined with a communion in the sacraments, of which the Eucharist rightly has received the name *Holy Communion*. There is also a communion in the graces and charisms 'which are given by the Spirit for the common good' (ICor 12,7) and a communion of charity 'which does not insist on its own' (I Cor 13,5), but which comes to the aid of the neighbour who is in want.

RC 1,10
24

The communion of the Church in heaven and on earth

954 Here on earth we are pilgrims. Those who have died are being purified, or have achieved that glory which God has reserved for those who love him: 'We all sing the one hymn of glory to God'.

LG 49

957 We do not simply venerate the memory of the saints in heaven, we seek rather by our devotion to strengthen the communion of the Church itself by our love for those who have shown their love for God, particularly the martyrs. We ask them to intercede for us with the Father, with the merits that they won by their lives on earth.

LG 50

S Polycarp
mart. 17

958 In turn, we intercede for those we call the *Holy Souls* in Purgatory, who are united with us in the family of the faith, 'that they might be delivered from their sins' (2 Mac 12,45).

LG 51

Mary – mother of Christ, mother of the Church

Mary's maternity

964 The union of Mary with her Son in the work of salvation unfolds from the very moment of her conception, until the hour of his passion, where she stood beneath the Cross, and his death. She also assisted the early Church with her prayers from the time of the Ascension and at

LG 57
LG 58
LG59

the end of her life shared in the Resurrection   Pius X
of her Son in a unique way by being assumed   DS 3903
body and soul into heaven (=*Assumption or
dormition*).

Mary is regarded, because of her unique dignity
and her abundant grace, as a wholly unique
member of the Church and its exemplar, model   LG 53
and perfect realisation. Because of her total   LG 63
obedience, her faith, hope and charity, she
cooperated in a wonderful way in the work of her   LG 61
Son and for this reason is, in the order of grace,
our mother. The Fathers of the Church explain
Christ's words to John from the cross, as his gift
to the Church of his mother 'Son behold your
mother!' (Jn 19,27). The Church invokes her also
as Advocate, Helper, Benefactress and Mediatrix.   LG 62

The cult of Mary

971   Mary has been honoured from earliest years under
the title of *Mother of God* by those who implored
her help and sought her intercession, praying to
her not to despise their petitions in their
necessities, but to deliver them from all dangers,
'O ever glorious and blessed Virgin'. Truly all
generations have called her blessed (Lk 1,48) and
we can trace this in the many liturgical feasts in her
honour, and in Marian devotions especially the
Angelus and the *Rosary*. Mary is also a sign of
certain hope and consolation and the image and
beginning of the Church as it is to be perfected in
the world to come.   LG 68

§3 The Forgiveness of Sins

One baptism for the forgiveness of sins

977   Baptism is the first and chief sacrament by which
our sins are forgiven, for 'we were buried
therefore with him by baptism into death, so that
as Christ was raised from the dead by the glory of
the Father, we too might walk in newness of life'
(Rom 6,4). It is through faith and the power of
baptism that we are freed from our sins, and such   Mk 16,
grace is so abundant that no sin, original or   15 – 16

actual, whether by commission or omission, RC 1,11,2
remains to be effaced, nor penalty to be expiated.

978   But the grace of baptism does not exempt us from
      the *effects of concupiscence* which subtly incline
      us towards sin. Therefore the Church needs to call
      on that power entrusted to her with the keys of the
      kingdom, to forgive other sins through that
      further sacrament of Penance.(q.v.)

The power of the keys

981   Christ not only commanded his apostles to baptize
      but also stated 'that repentance and forgiveness of
      sins should be preached in his name to all nations'
      (Lk 24,47). Peter fulfils these words when he tells
      the crowd on the day of Pentecost, 'Repent and be
      baptized every one of you in the name of Jesus
      Christ for the forgiveness of your sins' (Acts
      2,38). This ministry of reconciliation is received   2 Cor 5,18
      by the apostles with the gift of the keys and the gift
      of the Holy Spirit .'He breathed on them and said,
      "Receive the Holy Spirit, whose sins you forgive,
      they are forgiven, whose sins you retain, they are
      retained"' (Jn 20,22−23). This power, which is
      given to the bishops and priests of the Church,
      extends to every sin however grave, so that
      nobody need despair of being forgiven, not just
      'seven times, but till seventy times seven' (Mt
      18,21).   RC 1,11,3

§4 *The Resurrection of the Body*

990   The term 'body' (*flesh* in Latin) refers to our
      mortal humanity, and its resurrection means that
      we shall rise to life as complete persons, body and
      soul, 'when death is swallowed up in victory'
      (I Cor 15,54).

989   We believe that since Christ is truly risen from the
      dead, then 'if the Spirit of him who raised Christ
      Jesus from the dead dwells in (us), he who raised
      Christ Jesus from the dead will give life to (our)
      mortal bodies also through his Spirit who dwells in
      (us)' (Rom 8,11). He is the first fruits of those who

have fallen asleep in death and in fact if Christ had
not been raised, our faith would be futile and we
would be still in our sins.   I Cor 15,17

992 The resurrection of the dead was a truth revealed
     progressively to the People of God. It was
     founded on faith in God the Creator of the whole
     person, body and soul, as well as on his enduring
     faithfulness to Abraham and his descendants: 'He
     is not God of the dead but of the living, for to him
     all are alive' (Lk 20,38).

     It was graphically expressed in the faith of the
     seven brothers at the time of the Maccabean   2 Mac
     revolt. Jesus told the Sadducees, who denied the 7,9.14
     fact, that they neither knew the Scriptures, nor the
     power of God. The same comment could be made   Mk 12,24
     to those who talk of a *spiritual* resurrection which
     leaves the body on one side of the grave, whereas
     Christ who is the resurrection and the life, the true
     temple of God promises to lose nothing given to   Jn 11,25
     Him by the Father but will raise it up at the last Jn 2,19–22
     day.   Jn 6,39–40

How are the dead raised?

997 S. Paul branded as foolishness those who asked
     'how are the dead raised? With what kind of a
     body do they come?' (I Cor 15,35) He pointed out
     that God gives a new body which is as different
     from, and yet as similar to the original, as a flower
     is to the seed from which it is sown: 'what is sown
     is perishable, what is raised is imperishable ... It
     is sown in weakness, it is raised in power' (I Cor
     15,42–43).

999 Christ came back to life with his own body; he was   Jn 20,26
     not a ghost, 'See my hands and my feet, that it is
     I myself; handle me and see; for a spirit has not
     flesh and bones as you see that I have' (Lk 24,39).
     Yet at the same time it was a body possessed of
     different properties and one which was not
     instantly recognisable, because it had entered
     into glory; and he will change 'our lowly body to
     be like his glorious body, by the power which
     enables him even to subject all things to himself'

(Phil 3,21). This heavenly life in the risen Christ is anticipated in this life, in our sharing in the Holy Eucharist. For if we live in Him and for Him, our life is hidden with Christ in God, and when Christ, who is our life appears, then we also will appear   Col 3,3
with Him in glory, as will those who have done evil   Col 3,4
and will rise to the resurrection of judgement.   Jn 5,29

Death

1006   Death brings to an end our mortal life and is a reminder of the transitory nature of all things 'because man goes to his eternal home ... and the dust returns to the earth as it was, and the spirit returns to God who gave it' (Eccl 12,5.7). Scripture tells us that death entered the world through sin, hence the last *enemy* to be destroyed is death. But for those who die in the grace of   Rom 6,23
Christ, death is that calm surrender to our   I Cor 15,26
Father's loving will which has been transformed   GS 18
by Christ's own death and entry into glory.   Lk 2,26

1010   The Church sees in death, that consummation which is begun in baptism and is necessary if we are to live that new life, so it can be considered in one sense an advantage, prompting a desire to   Phil 1,21
depart to be with Christ. In the Liturgy of the Dead the Church reminds us 'that for your faithful, Lord, life is changed, not taken away; and when this earthly dwelling place is destroyed, an eternal home awaits us in heaven'.

1013   For man there will be no return to this world, for we only die once and therefore we pray to be   Heb 9,27
delivered from a sudden and unforeseen death and   Litany of
ask Jesus, Mary and Joseph to intercede for us,   Saints
that God in his mercy may grant us a safe lodging,   Newman
a holy rest, and peace at last.   SD 307

§5 *Everlasting Life*

1020   Death for the Christian is the gate to eternal life, which the Church holds before the dying person who has been given absolution, the anointing of the sick, *viaticum* for that last journey and the plenary papal indulgence:

'Go forth, O Christian soul, out of this world, in the name of God the Father Almighty, who created you; in the name of Jesus Christ, the Son of the living God who suffered for you; in the name of the Holy Spirit, who was poured out upon you; may you take your place today in peace and make your home with God in holy Zion with Mary the Virgin Mother of God, S. Joseph and all the angels and saints of God ... Return to the Creator who formed you from the dust of the earth, and when your soul leaves your body, may Mary and all the saints come to meet you ... May you see your Redeemer face to face.'

1021　At death comes the night when no one can work out their salvation any more, but must admit to being judged according to their works 'for what will it profit a man if he gains the whole world and loses his life? What shall a man give in return for his life?' (Mt 16,26) We must answer to Christ, to whom all judgement has been given by the Father, for the reward or punishment or purification which is be accepted by our immortal soul. `Jn 5,22`

Heaven

1023　The destiny of those made perfect in love is to see God face to face, not through a mirror, but 'as he is' (I Jn 3,2). This is the *beatific vision*. In 1336 Pope Benedict XII solemnly defined that 'the souls of the saints who departed this world before the Passion of our Lord Jesus Christ and all those ... who died after receiving the holy baptism of Christ — provided that they had no need of purification at the time of their death, or will not have such need when they die at some future time ... even before the resurrection of their bodies and the last Judgement ... have seen and do see the divine essence with an intuitive and even face-to-face vision, without the interposition of any creature; rather the divine essence manifests itself to them plainly, clearly and openly. The same thing is true of the souls of children who have been reborn in baptism and of those still to be baptized after they shall have been baptized, when they die before attaining the use of free will'. `Benedictus Deus DS 1000` `LG 49`

1026 By his death, Christ opened heaven for us, where there will be 'no more sadness, nor crying, nor pain any more, for the former things have passed away' (Rev 21,4). Scripture cannot describe such eternal happiness except to talk in terms of light, life, peace, the heavenly Jerusalem, the wedding banquet, our Father's house, paradise, the wine of the kingdom which 'eye has not seen, nor ear heard, nor has it entered into the heart of man, these things which God has prepared for those who love Him' (I Cor 2,9). In the glory of heaven there will be that continuing joy of seeing God's plan for creation unfold in eternity, 'There we shall rest and we shall love and we shall praise. This is what shall be in the end without end'.

Mt 25,21f
Rev 22,5
Aug civ Dei 22,30,1

Purgatory or the final purification

1030 S. John of the Cross says that in the evening of our life we will be examined in love and certainly the suffering of those who are not sufficiently holy to enter heaven is far distinct from the punishment of the damned. Scripture compares its cleansing effect to that of fire which burns out all impurities from base metal.

Sayings 57
Flo
DS 1304
Trent
DS 1580
1 Cor 3,13f

1032 Already in the Old Testament we find evidence of the value placed on intercession for the dead: 'it was a holy and pious thought. Therefore he (Judas Maccabeus) made atonement for the dead, that they might be delivered from their sin' (2 Mac 12,45). The Church has always taught that intercession (*suffragia*) for the faithful departed does assist in their release from purgatory, especially the sacrifice of the Mass, but also indulgences applied to them, penance, almsgiving and prayers. The month of November is set aside to commemorate them.

Trent
DS 1820

Hell

1033 There is the terrible reality of rejecting the merciful love of God and dying unrepentant in one's sin. Anyone who makes this free choice at the end of his life separates himself from communion with God in the eternal fire of hell.

1035   This is not a cleansing, but rather that punishing flame which resembles a gnawing pain where 'their worm does not die, and the fire is not quenched' (Mk 9,48).

1034   Jesus frequently referred to that unending fire of *gehenna* reserved for those who refused to repent and risked losing both body and soul, hearing at the end those terrible words 'Depart from me, you cursed, into the eternal fire prepared for the devil and his angels' (Mt 25,41).   Mt 5, 22.29   Mt 10,28   Mt 13, 41–42

1036   At the same time, the existence of Hell provides an urgent motive for conversion while time remains: 'Enter by the narrow gate; for the gate is wide and the way is easy, that leads to perdition, and those who enter it are many. For the gate is narrow and the way is hard that leads to life, and those who find it are few' (Mt 7,13–14).

1037   God never predestines anyone to Hell. Indeed he does not wish any to perish 'but that all should reach repentance' (2 Pt 3,9). At every Mass the Church prays that we may be saved from final damnation and counted among God's chosen ones.   DS 397   DS 1567   MR   EP I. 88

The last judgement

1038   All judgement has been given into his hands by the Father and he will reveal the truth about every person's life, the good they have done and the evil they have inflicted: 'for the hour is coming when all who are in the tombs will hear his voice and come forth, those who have done good, to the resurrection of life, and those who have done evil, to the resurrection of judgement' (John 5,28–29). There will be that final and public reckoning: 'and I saw the dead, great and small, standing before the throne, and books were opened ... And the dead were judged by what was written in the books, by what they had done' (Rev 20,12). It will coincide with that glorious return of Christ escorted by his angels, which we await with hope because we know neither the day nor the hour.   2 Thes 1,1   Mt 25,31f   Mt 25,13

The hope of new heavens and a new earth

1042 The final accomplishment of God's plan is the   GS 48
transformation of this world, which Scripture
calls 'new heavens and a new earth in which
righteousness dwells' (2 Pt 3,13). It will involve
the recapitulation of creation itself, in which all
things were made through Christ, and which will
now be united in him, 'things in heaven and things
on earth', (Eph 1,10), 'for the former things have
passed away' (Rev 21,4).

1044 In this heavenly city, 'prepared as a bride adorned
for her husband' (Rev 21,2) the harmony of
paradise will be restored, as sin and selfishness will   GS 39
be banished for ever and 'creation will be set free
from its bondage to decay' (Rom 8,21) so that
God will be 'all in all' (I Cor 15,28).

'Amen'

1061 The Hebrew word 'Amen' has the same root as the
word 'believe'. Thus in Isaiah, the God of Truth is   Is 65,16
the God of the Amen. When we believe we say in
fact "Amen" to the promises of God and his
faithfulness to us his People, which find their
fulfilment in his Son, 'for all the promises of God
find their 'Yes' in him. That is why we utter the
Amen through him to the glory of God' (2 Cor
1,20).

Part Two
The Celebration of the Christian Mystery

I The Liturgy

1066 In the Creed, the Church professes its faith in that mystery 'hidden from eternity in God who created all things' (Eph 3,9) which is accomplished in the gift of his son and the Holy Spirit for the salvation of the world and the glory of his name.

1067 Christ fulfilled this work of redemption principally by the Paschal mystery of his blessed passion and resurrection, his descent among the dead and his glorious ascension for 'by dying he destroyed our death and by rising he restored our life'. It is this mystery which the Church proclaims and celebrates in her liturgy. **SC 2**

1069 The word *liturgy* originally meant the service performed by an individual for the state (*leitourgía*) and, by derivation, as service to God. Through the liturgy Christ, our great High Priest and our 'minister in the sanctuary' (Heb 8,2) continues in the Church, with her and for her, the work of our redemption. **Jn 17,4**

1071 The Church, sharing in the liturgy of Christ, continues his priestly office through the worship which she offers, his prophetic office in the proclamation of the Gospel and his royal office in the practice of charity. It also offers that prayer of Christ which is addressed to the Father in the Holy Spirit in which all Christian prayer is rooted. **SC 7** **Acts 13** **Rom 15,** **Rom 15,** **Eph 3,16**
　　'The liturgy is the summit towards which all the activity of the Church is directed and from which at the same time, all her strength flows.' **SC 10**

Chapter 1: The Sacramental Economy

The dispensation or communication of the fruits of the paschal mystery in the celebration of the Church's liturgy.

The paschal mystery

1077 a) The paschal mystery is a work of the whole Trinity, because in the first place it is a response in faith and love to the spiritual blessings which have been poured out on creation by the Father from the time of paradise through to the age of Abraham and Noah, the birth of Isaac, the Passover, the gift of the Promised Land, the presence of God in the Temple, the exile and homecoming, together with the Law, the prophecies and the psalms. At the same time it is that return which the Church makes for all it has been given 'to the praise of his glorious grace' (Eph 1,6).

1084 b) In the second place, in the liturgy Christ, having died once for sin, dies now no more but all that he did and suffered remains forever present, since he *lives* to intercede for us. He is present in the apostles and their successors with his power of sanctification, and he is present in the sacraments, particularly the Sacrifice of the Mass in which we have a foretaste of that heavenly liturgy where Christ sits at the right hand of God as minister of the sanctuary and true tabernacle. — Rom 6,10 / Heb 7,27 / Rom 8,34 / LG 50 / SC 8

1091 c) Thirdly, the Holy Spirit acts in the Church as he acts in former times in the history of salvation. He prepares the Church to meet Christ. He calls Christ to mind and makes him known to the assembly at one and the same time and actually brings about his presence by his power as well as uniting the whole community together in Christ's life and mission.

* *The Holy Spirit prepares the Church to meet Christ*

1093 This preparation is above all through the salvation history of the Old Testament in its reading of the Law, the prophets, the writings and the psalms, seeing the connection between the events of significance such as the promise and the covenant, exodus and the passover, the kingdom and the

Temple, the exile and the return. All this is fulfilled in Christ, who allows us to see a hidden spiritual meaning in the happenings, words and symbols of the Old Covenant which come to light in the New.

1095   For this reason, the Church especially during Advent and Lent and the Easter Vigil reads the great events of salvation history and sees them as having a fulfilment in the Church of our day.

1096   The structure of the Christian liturgy is based on Jewish forms of worship, in particular it follows the place of Scripture, the responses and the whole Liturgy of the word with its prayers of praise and intercession for the living and the dead and its invocation of the mercy of God. The Liturgy of the Hours, the Prayer over the gifts and Holy Water find their origin here, as do the Eucharistic Prayers and the Our Father, Benedictus and Magnificat. The Church's calendar is strongly influenced by the great festivals of the Chosen People, in particular Passover and Pentecost; yet whereas for the Jews Passover looks towards the coming Messiah, for the Church it is the celebration of His death and resurrection.

* The Holy Spirit calls the mystery of Christ to mind

1099   The Holy Spirit is promised to the Church to bring to mind all that Christ has said, which is accomplished firstly through making the Scriptures find a response in the hearts of those who listen and then to awaken the memory of what Christ has done, so giving rise to thanksgiving and praise (Doxology).   Jn 14,26   SC 24   PO 4

* The Holy Spirit brings about the presence of Christ

1104   The transforming power of the Holy Spirit by invocation (*epiclesis*) of the Father − on the oil, the person to be ordained and the bread and wine − is integral to the presence of Christ in power, or in Person. The Holy Spirit makes present that one and unique mystery of Christ.

The Paschal Mystery in the Sacraments of the Church

The Sacraments of Christ

1114   The Church professes that all the Sacraments of the new law have been instituted by Our Lord Jesus Christ. We are told that during his life 'the power of the Lord was with him' (Lk 5,17) and that power, indeed 'all that was visible in our Saviour has passed into his sacraments'.

Trent
DS 1601

Leo I
Serm 74,2

The Sacraments of the Church

1117   The Church in the course of centuries has determined that there are seven liturgical celebrations which are strictly termed sacraments. It is the sacraments which create the Church because they reveal to mankind the mystery of that communion which is the Trinity.

Trent
DS 1601

The Sacraments of faith

1122   An old adage says '*lex orandi, lex credendi*', the law of prayer is the law of faith. The Church believes as it prays. The sacraments do not only presuppose faith, but by words and signs nourish, strengthen and express it. Therefore no one, either individually or as a community, can modify the sacramental rites on their own initiative.

SC 59

The Sacraments of salvation

1127   If the sacraments are celebrated worthily they confer the grace which they signify. They have an efficacy because it is Christ who baptises, Christ who forgives. They act therefore *ex opere operato* (by the action itself) in virtue of the saving work of Christ, accomplished once for all. Provided that a sacrament is celebrated in conformity with the intention of the Church, the power of Christ and his Holy Spirit act in and through the minister, independently of his personal worthiness. The fruitfulness of the sacraments does however depend on the dispositions of the one who receives.

Aquinas
ST 3,68,8

1129 The sacraments are necessary for our salvation and there is a sacramental grace proper to each which prepares us for that inheritance which we hope for when it reaches its fulfilment in the kingdom of heaven.

Trent
DS 1605

Lk 22,15f

Chapter 2: The Celebration of the Liturgy

1137 *The Celebrants* of the liturgy in heaven are the Lord God and the Lamb (who is Christ crucified and risen), great priest of the true sanctuary; and the Holy Spirit, that 'water of life, bright as crystal, flowing from the throne of God and of the Lamb' (Rev 22,4) as well as the powers of heaven and that immense multitude who serve God from every nation, from all tribes and peoples and tongues, standing before the throne and before the Lamb ... and crying out 'Salvation belongs to our God who sits upon the throne, and to the Lamb' (Rev 7,9–10). While on earth the members of the Church share in that perfect work of praise which Christ offers to the Father as our great High Priest enabling us to offer through the ministry of the priesthood, as one body, that living sacrifice holy and acceptable to God. Each share in the celebration in different ways, depending on their orders and the functions they perform. The ordained minister is considered an *icon* of Christ the priest, who acts in the person of Christ the Head in the service of all the members of the Body which is the Church. Others such as lectors and acolytes are called to a true ministry, and servers, readers, commentators and the choir have their part to play in the liturgy. Each should carry out *all and only* those parts which pertain to him by virtue of the function he performs and the principles of the liturgy.

Is 6,1
Rev 5,6
Heb 10,19

Rev 4–5
Heb 12,

LG 10
Rom 12,1

Rom 12,4
SC 27

SC 29
SC 28

Component parts of the liturgy

1145 Certain *signs and symbols* (which are found in all great religions and are part of our ordinary language, i.e. washing, breaking bread) are essential to the liturgy. Some signs stem from the Covenant itself such as circumcision, the

anointing of kings and priests, the imposition of
hands and sacrifices, especially that of the
passover. These are anticipations of the sacraments. Jesus often used signs and symbolic actions   Jn 9,6
to reveal the mysteries of the kingdom and heal the   Lk 8,10
sick. The Church possesses in the sacraments   Jn 9,6
certain signs and symbols, which through the Holy
Spirit signify and bring about the salvation of
Christ and anticipate the life of heaven.

1153   *Words and actions* accompany the signs and are
integral parts of the celebration. They help to
reveal the wonders of God and express the faith of   Mt 21,15
the Church which responds. The liturgy of the
word itself should be surrounded with a certain
solemnity: procession, incense, candles, and this
should extend to the actual lectionary or Book of
the Gospels, the ambo, the proclamation of the
words themselves and the responsorial psalms and
acclamation and the homily that follows. It is
right that such passages should be sung in
accordance with the tradition of the early Church,
'in psalms and hymns and spiritual songs, singing
and making melody to the Lord with all your   Ps 72,1
heart' (Eph 5,19), for according to S. Augustine,
he who sings, prays twice. Such chant should be
closely connected with the action of the liturgy   SC 112
responding to the moments where a response is
called for, such as the acclamations. The whole
effect should lift up the mind and heart and if use
is made of local hymns and musical traditions,
they should be in conformity with Catholic
doctrine with a firm basis in Scripture and the   SC 119
liturgical sources.   SC 121

Sacred images

1159   Because the only Son of God has made known the
splendour of the Father, the words of Christ have   Nic II
been complemented by images of him. The   DS 600
pictures and statues of the Mother of God, the
angels and the saints draw us towards the glory of
God which is manifested in them. As *icons* they
proclaim our faith and stimulate our prayer so
that we are caught up in a love of the world which
we cannot see.   I Jn 3,2

Sacred time

1163 The Church listens to the voice of Scripture urging: 'Today, when you hear his voice, harden not your hearts', but rather 'strive to enter that sabbath rest' which is the hour of the passover of Christ. For us, the focus and centre of the liturgy is the paschal mystery of the passion, death, resurrection and ascension. *Sunday* is that weekly reminder of the day of the Lord's resurrection which is made holy by our celebration of the Eucharist. *The liturgical year* revolves around the feast of Easter, the solemnity of solemnities, the Great Sunday, as Athanasius called it. In the East Holy Week is called the Great Week. The whole year unfolds in a certain way from Easter, the Advent and Christmas cycle being the beginnings of the paschal mystery.

Heb 3,7,11

SC 102
SC 106

Ep fest 329

1170 The Council of Nicea in 325 agreed that Easter should be celebrated in all churches on the Sunday following the full moon (14 Nisan) after the Spring equinox. The Gregorian reform of the calendar in 1582 has meant that there is a time lapse between Eastern and Western celebrations of Easter. Attempts are being made to bring about a common agreement and possibly a fixed date each year.

1172 During the year the Church also venerates the various mysteries of Our Lady, the perfect work of God's salvation and the fruit of his redemption, as well as the martyrs and saints who are our examples of faith and who by their merits obtain for us the blessings of God.

SC 103

SC 104

The Liturgy of the Hours

1174 The public prayer of the Church, or 'Divine Office', is that fulfilment of the command to pray without ceasing, for throughout the day at various times, praise goes up to God. The readings from Scripture and the Fathers help in the understanding of the psalms which are the basic constituent; and the whole is a stimulus to private prayer and a prolongation of the Eucharist.

1175   Priests are obliged to recite the Liturgy of the   PO 5
Hours as men of prayer, and servants of God's   SC 98
word; religious, because of their consecrated life,
should recite certain portions; it is recommended
that there should be public recitation with the laity
in Church especially on Sundays and principal
feast days, or that the laity should be encouraged
to pray the Hours in private.   SC 100

The house of God

1179   When Jacob was aware of the presence of God
after he had dreamed of the ladder reaching to
heaven, he awoke and said 'How awesome is this
place! This is none other than the house of God,
this is the gate of heaven' (Gen 28,17). Our
churches are not simply meeting places, but, by   SC 122–7
their design and beauty they must reveal to all,
that dwelling-place of God where 'living stones
(are) built up into a spiritual house' (I Pt 2,5). The
house of God must therefore reveal that Christ is
present and acts there.   SC 7

1182   *The tabernacle* should be in the most prominent
place since the eucharist is the spiritual centre of
the universal Church, the Lord really present
among us. It should be secure as well as truly
dignified.

The chrism (*myron*) is traditionally kept in an
aumbry on the sanctuary. There also can be
kept the oils of the sick and of catechumens.

The presidential chair must be worthy of the
one who presides and directs the prayers of the
community.

The ambo to allow the proclamation of the
word of God.

The baptistery and *holy water font* should be
part of every Church.

Confessionals or *confession rooms* to allow the
faithful in secrecy to approach the sacrament of
penance.

Different liturgical traditions

1202 Within the Catholic Church there is a great diversity of tradition, within the one faith. The Latin rite includes within it the *Ambrosian* and *Mozarabic* rites and the Eastern Church has Byzantine, Alexandrine or Coptic, Syriac, Armenian, Maronite and Chaldean rites. The Church wishes to preserve these and foster them. SC 4

II The Seven Sacraments of the Church

Chapter 1: The Sacraments of Initiation

1210   There is a certain analogy between sharing the divine life and the beginning, growth and support of natural life. We are born to new life in baptism, strengthened by Confirmation and receive the Bread of Life in the Eucharist.

The sacrament of Baptism

1213   The basis of the whole of the Christian life, the gate which opens on to the other sacraments (*vitae spiritualis ianua*). We are freed from sin by this sacrament and reborn as sons of God and members of the Church. Baptism is the sacrament of regeneration by water and the word.

Flo
DS 1314
CIC 204

RC 2,2,5

The various names which describe the Sacrament

1214   *Baptism* means to plunge or immerse (*baptizein*) in water. It symbolises going down into the grave with Christ so as to rise with Him to new life. It is also called the *washing of regeneration* (Tit 3,5), *illumination*, or *enlightenment*, because the Word is the true light which enlightens all mankind and the one who is baptized becomes light, and son of the light.

Rom 6,4
Col 2,12
Jn 1,9
Eph 5,8
1 Thes 5,5

Baptism foreshadowed in the Old Testament

1217   In the beginning Scripture tells us that the Spirit of God moved *over the waters* so that they might teem with life. This is recalled in the Easter Vigil in the blessing of the font. Later, the ark of Noah was seen as a sign of the salvation by baptism 'in which a few, that is eight persons, were saved through water' (I Pt 3,20). But it is the crossing of the Red Sea into the freedom of the Promised Land which prefigures the freeing from sin in baptism.

Gen 1,2
MR Vigil 42

The Baptism of Christ

1223   Our Lord freely submitted to John's baptism to   Mt 3, 1
fulfil all righteousness and to take on the burden   Mt 3,
of sin, but the appearance of the Spirit and the   16–17
voice of the Father already proclaim the beginning
of that new creation in which all become beloved
sons of God. This was accomplished in that
passover with which Christ longed to be baptised,
and the Fathers see in the blood and water flowing
from his side on the Cross, the sacraments of   Mk 10,38
baptism and the Eucharist, the new life of the   Lk 12,50
members of the Church.   Jn 19,34

Baptism in the Church

1226   Christ's command to make disciples of all
nations, baptising them in the name of the Father,
the Son and of the Holy Spirit was put into effect
on the very day of Pentecost as the direct response
to belief in Jesus as the Son of God: 'Believe in the
Lord Jesus, and you will be saved . . . and he was   Mt 28,19
baptised at once with all his family' (Acts   Acts 2,38
16,31,33). Those who are baptised put on Christ   Gal 3,27
and are washed, sanctified and justified.   I Cor 6,11

The Celebration of the Sacrament of Baptism

1230   Christian initiation has varied in its long history,
but began with a long catechumenate which
finally concluded with the reception of the
sacraments of initiation. Children were baptised
in a rite which telescoped the process, but this was
compensated for by post-baptismal catechesis: the
catechism. The Second Vatican Council restored
the catechumenate and published the *Rite of the
Christian Initiation of Adults* in 1972.

1234   The meaning and grace of the sacrament of
Baptism is revealed through the rites themselves.

The sign of the Cross is the mark of Christ on one
who is going to belong to him by the redemption
won by him on the Cross.

The Proclamation of God's Word is designed to

evoke the faith of the parents, godparents and congregation, joined as it is with a homily on the importance of this entry into the life of faith.

The *exorcisms* signify the casting out of sin and its instigator the devil, who is renounced with all his works so that one can be strengthened with the *oil of catechumens* in the name of Christ our Saviour.   2 Thes 3,3

The profession of faith is that Symbol or Creed that is the faith of Christians into which each is baptised.

The baptismal water is blessed by an invocation of the Holy Spirit (either at the time or during the Easter Vigil), so that the water may receive the power of sanctifying those who are born of water and the Holy Spirit.   Jn 3,5

The Baptism takes place by a three-fold pouring of water (or three-fold immersion) while the minister says *N, I baptise you in the Name of the Father and of the Son, and of the Holy Spirit.*

1240   In the oriental rites, the catechumen faces the East and the priest says 'The servant of God, N, is baptised in the Name of the Father, and of the Son, and of the Holy Spirit', and at each invocation, he immerses him once in the water.

The Anointing with Chrism signifies the gift of the Holy Spirit. One who is baptised is anointed by the Holy Spirit and puts on Christ who is anointed priest, prophet and king.

The white garment symbolises that resurrection from sin and that clothing with the new life of Christ, the wedding garment of the kingdom of God, which recalls the innocence of our first parents. [The celebrant at Mass recalls these realities when he puts on the *alb*.] *The candle,* lit from the paschal candle, symbolises that the baptised is enlightened by Christ, the light of the world, to be a light in his or her turn.   Col 3,9
Gal 3,27
Ambrose
Myst 34

Mt 5,14–16

The Our Father is the natural prayer of the one who is now the child of God and who has received the spirit of sonship to say 'Abba! Father!' The Spirit himself bears witness with our spirit that we are children of God.   I Jn 3,1
Rom 8,15.

The Blessings, while thanking God for the gift of new life, also refer to the faith that is passed on by the parents to the child.   LG 11

The Baptism of children

1247   The gratuity of God's grace is seen most particularly in the baptism of children, because everyone born into the world needs to be delivered   Col 1,13 from darkness and transferred to the kingdom of the beloved Son of God, with all sin forgiven. Children should be baptised soon after birth. Such   CIC 857 a practice is attested from the second century, but   Acts 16,15 the very fact that the apostolic writings speak of   Acts 16,33 the baptism of entire houses leads us to infer that   Acts 18,8 children were.   1 Cor 1,16

Faith and Baptism

1253   'What do you ask of the Church of God?', the catechumen or godparent is asked, and the reply is, 'Faith!' baptism is *into* the faith of the Church and everyone's faith needs to grow. This is the reason for the renewal of baptismal promises every Easter Vigil, and shows the importance of the godparent having a special function in the Church, to reinforce the resolve of the parents in bringing up the child in the faith of the Church.

Who can baptise?

1256   The ordinary ministers of baptism are the bishop, the priest, and in the Latin Church, the deacon. In   CIC 872–4 a case of urgency anyone, even someone who is not baptised, can baptise, provided that there is the intention of doing what the Church performs in baptism and the Trinitarian formula is used. This provision flows from God's will that all should be saved.   I Tim 2,4

The necessity of Baptism

1257   Christ affirmed to Nicodemus 'Unless one is born of water and the Spirit, he cannot enter the kingdom of God' (Jn 3,5) and he emphasised this in his commands to the disciples to preach the

Gospel to all nations, that he who believes and is baptised will be saved. The Church's missionary activity is a response to that urgent command, by which Christ links salvation with the sacrament of baptism.

Mk 16,16

1258   Apart from Baptism *by water*, the Church has always believed that those who die for the faith, without receiving Baptism, are baptised by their death for and with Christ in a *baptism of blood*. Those catechumens who die before receiving the sacrament are said to receive the *baptism of desire*. Christ's command 'Let the children come to me, do not hinder them' (Mk 10,14) can also be applied to those children who die before receiving baptism, or are the victims of abortion. We are permitted to believe that God's mercy will not abandon them, but through the faith of the Church bring them his salvation.

The grace of Baptism

1263   *The Forgiveness of sins*: all sins, both original and actual and all the punishment due for sin. However, the consequences of sin remain, specifically concupiscence, pain, weakness and death; these remain so that we can obtain the crown of life by struggling against our weaknesses.

Flo
DS 1316
Trent
DS 1515
2 Tim 2,5

1265   *A New Creation*: 'If anyone is in Christ, he is a new creation' (2 Cor 5,17) by being adopted as a son of God and a sharer in the divine nature, a member of Christ, a fellow heir with Him and a temple of the Holy Spirit.
    * *Sanctifying Grace*, the grace of *justification*
        – makes us capable of believing and hoping in God and loving God with the *theological virtues* of faith, hope and charity.
        – gives us the power to live and act under the influence of the Holy Spirit by the *gifts of the Holy Spirit* (q.v.)
        – allows us to increase in goodness through the *moral virtues*. (q.v.)

The 'Character' of Baptism

1272   In Baptism we are conformed to the image of Christ in an indelible way. This is called the baptismal *character*. It cannot be removed by sin, even if sin prevents the fruitfulness of the sacrament from having its effect. Once given it cannot therefore be repeated. The *character* which we as Christians receive, consecrates us so that we can offer that perfect sacrifice of praise in the liturgy. It is that seal with which we are marked 'for the day of redemption' (Eph 4,30), so that marked with the sign of faith we may come to its consummation in heaven.   Rom 8,29 — Trent DS 1609–19 — LG 11 — LG 10 — MR EP I. 97

1271   Baptism is the sacramental bond which unites all Christians and is the basis for a certain, imperfect communion between separated Christians and the members of the Catholic Church.

The Sacrament of Confirmation

1285   This Sacrament is necessary to complete the grace given in Baptism. It also gives a special strength through the Holy Spirit to bear witness to Christ in a more determined way by word and action.   LG 11

Confirmation in the economy of salvation

1286   Isaiah prophesied that the Spirit of the Lord would rest on the Messiah that God would send to his Chosen People, recognised by John as 'He on whom you see the Spirit descend and remain' (Jn 1,32), who receives the Spirit 'in full measure' (Jn 3,34).   Is 11,2; 61,1 — Lk 4,16f

1287   The Spirit is also to be poured out on the whole messianic people. This is first realised on Easter Day and in a more spectacular way on the day of Pentecost, when Peter declares this to be the sign of the messianic age.   Ez 36,25f — Jl 3,1–2 — Lk 12,12 — Jn 3,5–8; 7,37–39; 16,7–15 — Acts 2.17

1288   By the imposition of hands the apostles fulfilled the will of Christ by bestowing upon the newly baptised the gift of the Spirit, the completion of the grace of Baptism. The Letter to the Hebrews emphasises this by Christian instruction 'about baptisms and the laying on of hands' (Heb 6,2). This imposition of hands is seen as perpetuating in the Church the grace of Pentecost. To this action was soon added an anointing with scented oil (*chrism*), to emphasise further that it is a gift of the Holy Spirit. It is called in the East, *chrismation* or *myron* (=chrism). The word *Confirmation* in the West suggests the strengthening of the grace received in Baptism.

1290   In the Western Church because of the desire to reserve the Sacrament to the Bishop, it became gradually separated from Baptism, whereas in the East the priest confirms with *myron* consecrated by the bishop. The Western practice brings into focus the communion of the new Christian with his bishop, guardian of the unity of the Church and of its catholicity and apostolic link with Christ and the Twelve.

The rite of Confirmation

1293   Anointing with oil is seen in the bible as having many meanings, it is a sign of consecration to God of kings, and priests; it is the sign of God's abundant blessings, and of joy of heart, it purified (before and after bathing). In the case of athletes, it made them supple and was a healing remedy for abrasions and wounds, so bringing grace, health and strength. All these aspects are found in the various oils used in the sacraments: *the oil of catechumens* used in Baptism stands for purification and strength; *the oil of the sick* is a sign of healing and comfort; *the anointing with chrism* is a sign of consecration by which we become the 'fragrance of Christ' (2 Cor 2,15) like the fragrant oil with which we have been anointed, allowing the Gospel of Christ to live in our words and our deeds.   Dt 11,14 / Ps 23,5; 104,15 / Is 1,6 / Lk 10,34

1295   By this anointing we are marked by the Holy Spirit, as soldiers were marked by the Emperor and slaves by their master, and by which documents are authenticated. Christ was marked by the seal of his Father and Christ in his turn 'has put his seal upon us and given us his Spirit in our hearts as a guarantee' (2 Cor 1,22).   Gen 38,18 / Gen 41,42 / Dt 32,34 / Jer 32,10 / Jn 6,27

The Celebration of Confirmation

1297 An important part of the ceremony is the previous consecration of the chrism on Maundy Thursday. In the Oriental Churches, this is reserved to the Patriarch, to illustrate its dignity.

1299 In the Latin rite, the bishop extends his hands over those who are to be confirmed and invokes the outpouring of the Holy Spirit to fill them with the fullness of the Spirit which rested on Christ, and the seven-fold gifts. The Sacrament is conferred by anointing the forehead with chrism, making the sign of the Cross and saying : 'N, be sealed with the gift of the Holy Spirit'. The Oriental Churches anoint the body in several places, saying each time 'Seal of the gift which is the Holy Spirit'. The rite ends with a ritual kiss of peace which symbolises the communion between the bishop and his flock.

The effects of Confirmation

1302 Confirmation is that full outpouring of the Holy Spirit, as on the day of Pentecost. It deepens in us our baptismal grace and therefore makes us more aware of our divine sonship. It unites us more firmly to Christ, increases in us the gifts of the Holy Spirit, binds us more perfectly to the Church and gives us the strength to be valiant witnesses to Christ and confessors of the faith.   LG 11 / VS 89

1304 As it is the completion of Baptism, it can only be received once.   Trent / DS 1609

The recipients of Confirmation

1306 All the baptised are bound to receive the sacrament at the appropriate time, with the age of discretion as the starting point, but even before if children are in danger of death. There should be catechesis so that the one to be confirmed can assume the responsibilities of an active Christian life in the parish and in the Church at large. One should be in a state of grace and have a sponsor who ought to be one of the godparents at Baptism.   CIC 890 / CIC 891

The minister

1312 The bishops are the original ministers of Confirmation. In the East, the priest who baptises confirms immediately afterwards, as part of the same celebration, but using the chrism consecrated by the patriarch or the bishop. This is the case in the Latin rite in adult baptisms, or when one admits a person from a separated Christian community into full communion.

LG 26

1313 In the Latin rite, the ordinary minister is the bishop. But he can grant the faculty to his priests for grave reasons. Every priest has this faculty if someone is in danger of death.

CIC 883
CIC 884
CIC 883

The Sacrament of the Eucharist

1322 The Eucharist marks the completion of Christian initiation. Those who are raised to the dignity of the royal priesthood by Baptism and bear that deeper likeness in Confirmation, share in the very sacrifice of Christ by means of the Eucharist. It is the very source and summit of the Christian life because it contains Christ Himself, our passover.

SC 47

LG 11
PO 5

The names given to this Sacrament

1328 *Eucharist (eucharistein* = to give thanks) so called because it is an act of thanksgiving to God and of blessing and praising him, who has created us, redeemed us, given us each day our daily bread and blessed us in Christ.

Lk 22,19
1 Cor 11,24
Mt 26,26
Mk 14,22
Eph 1,3

Lord's Supper because it is that Supper which Jesus took with his disciples the night before he suffered, and looks forward to that marriage supper of the Lamb in the heavenly Jerusalem.

Rev 19,9

Breaking of Bread because it was the gesture used by Christ which was recognised by his disciples after his resurrection, and has that further meaning, that all who eat of this broken Bread of life will form one Body with Him.

Mt 14,19
Mk 8,6.19
Lk 24,
13 – 35
1 Cor
10,16 – 17

Memorial because it commemorates the passion and resurrection of Christ.

Acts 2, 42.46
20,7.11.

Holy Sacrifice because it is that pure and holy sacrifice of praise which fulfils and surpasses all the sacrifices of the Old Testament.

Mal 1,11
Heb 13,15
Heb 9,24

Holy and divine Liturgy or *Holy Mysteries* are terms used especially in the Eastern Church, because the Eucharist is the central act to which all the liturgy tends.

Blessed Sacrament which refers to the eucharistic species reserved in the tabernacle, because it is the Sacrament of sacraments.

Communion

The Eucharist unites us in Christ to form one Body with Him. It is also called *viaticum* when given to the dying as well as *Bread of life* and *Bread of angels*.

1 Cor 10,
16 – 17

Holy Mass because the Liturgy concludes with the sending forth of the people (*missio*) into the world to live out their faith.

The Eucharist in the economy of salvation

1333   Already in the figure of Melchisedech, King of Salem who 'brought forth bread and wine' (Gen 14,18), the church sees that greater sacrifice. At the time of the Exodus bread and wine were given a deeper significance as they formed part of that yearly celebration of the passover — the unleavened bread recalling the hastiness of the departure. Later still there would be the reminder of the manna so that Israel might know 'that man does not live on bread alone' (Dt 8,3) while the cup of blessing at the end of the Passover would look forward to that final messianic banquet.

MR EP I.
95
Heb 7,1f

Ex 12,11.17

1 Cor 10,16

1335   When Jesus changed water into wine at Cana, he signified that the hour of his glorification was imminent when they would drink the new wine in the kingdom of God which would be his very blood. He had already announced after the multiplication of the loaves that he was the Bread of life 'and the bread which I shall give for the life of the world is my flesh' (Jn 6,51).

Mk 14,25

1336   The Eucharist was an obstacle for some at the beginning: 'This is a hard saying; who can listen to

it?' (Jn 6,60). It remains that scandal, like the
Cross itself, which demands a similar faith in
Christ who has the words of eternal life.   Jn 6,68.

The institution of the Eucharist

1337   We are told by S. John that 'when Jesus knew that
his hour had come to depart out of this world to
the Father, having loved his own who were in the
world, he loved them to the end' (Jn 13,1). The
pledge of that love was the Eucharist, the
memorial of his death and resurrection. The Last
Supper was the fulfilment of the passover in His   Lk 22,15
own Body and Blood, the new and everlasting   Mt 26,28
covenant.   Mk 14,24

1341   The command of Jesus to repeat his actions and
words in remembrance of him 'until he comes'   Lk 22,19
(I Cor 11,26) enshrines the order of priesthood   Trent
and the concept of apostolic succession.   DS 1740

The liturgical celebration of the Eucharist

1346   The structure of the celebration of the Eucharist in
the early Church was that of a liturgy of the word,
followed by a homily and prayers of intercession;   Justin
then the liturgy of the Eucharist, consisting of the Apol 1,65
presentation of the bread and wine, the prayer of
consecration and communion — both forming
one single act of worship. We can see this
foreshadowed in that meeting between the risen
Christ and the disciples on the road to Emmaus,
for first he opens the Scriptures to them and then
'He took the bread and blessed and broke it, and
gave it to them' (Lk 24,30).   SC 56

The parts of the Eucharistic Liturgy

1349   On Sundays and Holidays *the liturgy of the word*
comprises a reading from the Old Testament, one
from the 'memories of the apostles', the letters or
apostolic writings and the Gospel, followed by the
homily and the intercessions 'for all men, for
kings and for all who are in high positions' (1 Tim
2,1–2).

1350   *The presentation of the gifts or offertory* recalls
the action of Melchisedech and the gesture of
Christ 'who took bread and a cup'. The offering
of bread and wine has been accompanied from
earliest days with the personal offerings of the   Justin
congregation for those in need, which Paul called   Apol 1,67,6
'the contribution for the saints'.   1 Cor 16,1

The Anaphora or Eucharistic Prayer

1352   This begins with the *preface* in which the Church
gives thanks for the divine work of creation,
redemption and sanctification, which ends always
in the *Sanctus*, Holy, Holy, Holy God ... This is
followed by the *epiclesis* asking that the Father
send his Holy Spirit to sanctify these offerings so
that they can become the Body and Blood of his
beloved Son (the epiclesis in some rites, follows the
anamnesis). The *words of institution* said by the
celebrant make Christ sacramentally present on
the altar under the appearances of bread and wine,
as our sacrifice, offered once for all upon the
Cross. In the *anamnesis* the Church presents the
offering of His Son to the Father, calling to mind
the saving mysteries of his passion, death, resurrection and return in glory and in the *intercessions*
the Church prays for all those living and dead in
communion with the Pope, the bishop of the
diocese, the priests and deacons and all bishops
throughout the world.

The Communion

1355   In Holy Communion we receive Christ, our Bread
of Life and our chalice of salvation, given for the
life of the world.   Jn 6,51

The sacrifice which is also sacrament

1359   Christ allows the Church in the Eucharist to give
thanks to God for the work of creation, and
particularly for humanity, created in the image of
the Creator, but also for the gift of grace and
redemption. It is also the sacrifice in which we
praise the glory of God *through* Christ, *with*
Christ and *in* Christ.

The memorial sacrifice of Christ and of his body, the Church

1362   The Eucharist is the memorial of Christ's Passover, the renewal and sacramental offering of his one sacrifice which takes place in the liturgy of the Church, which is his Body.

1363   The concept of *memorial* for the people of Israel was not simply a remembrance of things past, but in a sense, a re-enactment of them each time the events were commemorated in the liturgical celebration. Thus in the Passover ritual cach ycar, the reality of the Exodus is made present to the believers who are gathered together.

1364   When the Church celebrates the Eucharist it remembers the Passover of Christ, who becomes present on the altar as our sacrifice. In the Eucharist Christ offers his body which was given up for us on the Cross, and the blood which was shed for many in remission of sins. It is one and the same sacrifice, for it is one and the same priest and victim: he who now makes the offering through the ministry of priests is he who then offered himself on the cross; the only difference being the manner of the offering.

LG 3

Trent
DS 1740

Mt 26,28

Trent
DS 1743

1368   The whole Church is united in the offering and intercession of Christ, as one Body, an everlasting gift to God, which includes the successor of Peter, the Pope, the local bishop, the clergy, those who are present and both those in heaven with Mary, the Mother of God and all the saints, and those who have gone to their rest, not yet wholly purified so that they may enter into their eternal home in heaven.

Heb 7,24f

The presence of Christ by the power of his word and the Holy Spirit

1373   The presence of Christ in the Blessed Sacrament is called *Real* because the Body, Blood, soul and divinity of Our Lord Jesus Christ are *truly*, *really* and *substantially* present, the whole Christ, God and man. This means that at the moment of

Trent
DS 1651
MF 39

consecration, the bread and wine are changed into the Body and Blood of Christ, so that nothing except the appearances of the former remain. The Catholic Church has fittingly and exactly named this *transubstantiation* because it is the change of one substance into another.

Trent
DS 1642

1378   The presence of Christ in the Eucharist remains as long as the appearances themselves, Christ being present whole and entire under either appearance and in every part. It has been the custom in the Church to venerate the Real Presence not simply during the Mass itself, but apart from the celebration, by taking the greatest care of consecrated hosts and by making visits to the Blessed Sacrament. Other Eucharistic devotions include the Solemnity of the Body and Blood of Christ, processions of the Blessed Sacrament, Exposition (including the *Forty Hours' Devotion*) and Eucharistic Congresses, of which *Benediction* (Blessing with the sacred host) forms a prominent part.

PV 48
CIC 938
MF 56

DC 3

The Paschal Banquet

1382   Our Lord urges us to receive him in Communion: 'Truly, truly I say to you, unless you eat the flesh of the Son of man and drink his blood, you have no life in you' (Jn 6,53). We approach this sacrament with deep respect; keeping the Eucharistic fast* prescribed by the Church together with that reverence of attitude and dress which remind us of the Sacrament we are to receive. If we are conscious of mortal sin we should go first to receive the Sacrament of Penance.

I Cor
11,27f

1389   The faithful are bound to take part in the Liturgy on Sundays and feastdays, and to receive Holy Communion at least once a year, and be prepared for this by the Sacrament of Penance. It is possible to receive Holy Communion twice in one day; and under both kinds (which is the habitual manner in the Oriental rites.)

OE 15
CIC 920

CIC 917

---

*One hour before the time of receiving Holy Communion; water does not break the fast.

1391   Among *the fruits of Communion* is a greater union with Christ, for He has told us that 'He who eats my flesh and drinks my blood abides in me and I in him. As the living Father sent me and I live because of the Father, so he who eats me will live because of me' (Jn 6,56–7). Our communion with the flesh of the risen Christ protects and increases the life of grace received in Baptism. At the same time it also purifies us from our daily faults and weaknesses which lead us into sin. As   Trent
       Holy Communion arouses the love of God   DS 1638
       strongly in us, it reduces in us the attraction of sin and draws us more closely into the Church where we are one Body in Christ.   1 Cor,10,16f

1399   The Eastern Churches which are not in com-   UR 15
       munion with Rome are united with us through   CIC 844
       apostolic succession and the Eucharist which makes a certain measure of intercommunion possible, subject to ecclesiastical approval; this is not possible with those Churches of the Reform that do not possess a true Eucharist, even though they do commemorate the death and resurrection of Christ in the celebration of the Lord's Supper.   UR 22

The Eucharist, pledge of the life to come

1402   In an ancient prayer, the Church professes her faith in the Eucharist: 'O sacred banquet, in which Christ is received, the memory of his passion renewed, the mind filled with grace, and a pledge of future glory is given to us.' Every time we receive the Eucharist we look forward to that glorious   Tit 2,13
       coming of the Son of man: 'Come, Lord Jesus'.   Rev 22,20

Chapter 2: The Sacraments of Healing

1420   We receive the treasure of the Christian life in the   2 Cor 4, 7
       sacraments of Initiation, but 'in earthen vessels'.   Lk 5, 17
       For this reason, because in Christ is the power to heal, he continues that power in his Church just as he sent out his apostles with authority. This is accomplished through the two sacraments, of Penance and The Anointing of the Sick.   Lk 9, 1

The Sacrament of Penance and Reconciliation

1422   The Sacrament of Penance is the action of God's mercy, pardoning those who sin against Him, and reconciling them to the Church which works for their conversion of heart.   LG 11

The names given to this Sacrament

1423   *Sacrament of penance* because it is the personal initiative of the penitent and the work of the Church to bring about repentance with a firm purpose of amendment.
Sacrament of conversion because it is the   Lk 15,18
sacramental response to Jesus' call to conversion, and to return to our Father's house.
Sacrament of confession both because the confession of sins to a priest is an integral part of the sacrament and because it is a 'confession' of the merciful nature of God towards the sinner.
Sacrament of pardon because through the absolution of the priest, the penitent is granted 'pardon and peace'.
Sacrament of reconciliation because it reconciles
us with God and through God's loving mercy we   2 Cor 5, 20
are ready to be reconciled with our brothers.   Mt 5, 24

The need for a Sacrament of Penance after Baptism

1425   In Baptism we have been forgiven our sins and made 'holy and immaculate in his sight' (Eph 1, 4). But the effects of sin still continue so that in S. John's words, 'If we say we have no sin, we
deceive ourselves' (1 Jn 1, 8). We have to struggle   Mk 1, 15
to overcome our fallen nature and listen to the   Acts 2, 38f
voice of Christ sounding in the Church calling us to conversion. For many, Baptism is the first result of that conversion, but there is also the
second conversion experienced by S. Peter. For in   Lk 22, 61
the Church there is, says S. Ambrose, 'water and tears: the water of Baptism and the tears of
Penance'.   Ep 41, 12

Inner repentance

1430   The Lord looks on the heart of man, calling for
that inner conversion which turns from sin with   Lam 5, 21
grief and sadness, because in sinning we have   RC 2, 5, 4
turned from the One who was sent by the Father.   Zch 12, 10
But the Holy Spirit who convicts the world of sin, Jn 16, 8–9
also gives to us that grace of conversion.   Jn 15, 26

The many forms of christian penance

1434   The three traditional forms of penance found in
Scripture and the Fathers are *prayer, fasting and*   Tob 12, 8
almsgiving. These summarise the conversion to   Mt 6, 1–18
God and towards one's neighbour. To this is
joined the practice of charity 'which covers a
multitude of sins' (I Pt 4, 8), the acceptance of the
Crosses of our daily life, spiritual direction, and
examination of conscience. We see the process   Lk 9,23
described for us graphically by Our Lord in the   Lk 15,
parable of the Prodigal Son. Holy Scripture,   11–24
prayed or recited in the Liturgy of the Hours,   Trent
arouses in us that spirit of penance, but the   DS 1638
Eucharist is our daily Bread to deliver us from evil. Mt 6, 13

1438   The Church sets aside Lent and every Friday as
times dedicated to the practice of penance, and
Ash Wednesday and Good Friday as days of
fasting and abstinence from meat.   CIC 1250

The Sacrament of Penance and Reconciliation

1441   God alone can forgive sins. That power Jesus   Mk 2, 7
claimed for himself, showing that he had power   Mk 2,10
also over the sickness of the body. He bestowed   Lk 7,48
that same power on his disciples after his
resurrection : 'As the Father has sent me, even so
I send you'. And when he had said this, he
breathed on them, and said to them, 'Receive the
Holy Spirit whose sins you shall forgive, they are
forgiven, whose sins you shall retain, they are
retained' (Jn 20, 21–23). The power of absolving
sin belongs to the successors of the apostles, the Mt 18,18;
bishops, who impart it to their priests, so that   28,16–20
through their ministry, sinners can be reconciled   LG 22
to God and the Church whom they have offended.   2 Cor 5,20

The development of the practice of the Sacrament of Penance

1447 * In the first centuries, grave sins, such as idolatry, adultery or murder were forgiven only after a rigorous penance lasting several years and was normally only conceded once in a lifetime.

* The Irish monks, inspired by Eastern monastic tradition introduced the practice of *private* penance in the 7th century which opened the way to a frequent reception of the sacrament and the confession of grave sins as well as weaknesses and other faults, which are named *venial* sins.

* The Church today demands that there should be on the part of the sinner, contrition, confession and penance (or satisfaction); and on the part of God and the Church, the absolution and the application of the penance.

The acts of the penitent

1450 *Contrition* is that 'deep sorrow and detestation for sin committed, with a resolve to sin no more'. If such sorrow stems from a total love of God it is called *perfect contrition*; if it is mixed with the feeling of shame for the sin committed and the fear of damnation, then it is *imperfect*. Perfect contrition forgives sin, but involves the intention of receiving absolution as soon as possible, whereas imperfect contrition does not forgive sin, and merely prompts one to seek absolution.
   Trent
   DS 1676
   Trent
   DS 1677 – 8

The practice of the *examination of conscience* is strongly recommended by saints and spiritual writers particularly before approaching the sacrament of Penance.

Confession of sins

1455 The admission of one's sins to a priest is an integral part of the sacrament. It extends to all mortal sins of which one is conscious, even those which are most secret and which only offend the first two commandments. The confession of daily faults/*venial* sins although not strictly necessary is strongly recommended by the Church because we
   Trent
   DS 1680

thereby receive the grace of God and the power of
the Holy Spirit to grow in that love which   CIC 988
overcomes the attraction of sin.
> *The words of absolution* are:
> God the Father of Mercies, through the
> death and resurrection of His Son, has
> reconciled the world to Himself and sent
> the Holy Spirit among us for the
> forgiveness of sins; through the ministry of
> the Church may God give you pardon and
> peace, and I absolve you from your sins in
> the name of the Father, and of the Son,
> and of the Holy Spirit. Amen.

1457   The faithful are bound to confess all mortal sins
once a year and if they have committed mortal sin,
cannot go to Communion, before they have
received sacramental absolution. They must not   Trent
presume simply to make an act of contrition,   DS 1680
unless there is a grave reason to receive   Trent
Communion and they cannot find a confessor.   DS 1647
Children should receive the sacrament of Penance   CIC 916
before they make their first Holy Communion.   CIC 914

Satisfaction or Penance

1459   Absolution forgives the sin but does not remedy
the causes of sin, and satisfaction or penance is a   Trent
means of recovering full spiritual health. The   DS 1712
penance helps to unite us especially with Christ
who is 'the expiation for our sins' (1 Jn 2, 2) and
allows us to bear some of the burden for the harm
they have caused.

The minister of the Sacrament of Penance

1461   Forgiveness of sins reconciles the sinner with God   CIC 844;
and with the Church. The bishop, the head of each   967 – 9;972
particular church, is therefore the chief minister
of the sacrament, 'the moderator of penitential   LG 26
discipline'. Priests are ministers by virtue of *the
faculty* they receive from their bishop (or religious
superior), or the Pope.

1463   Certain particularly grave sins make one subject
to excommunication, and their absolution is

reserved to the bishop or the Pope, or a priest authorised by them. In danger of death, every priest, even if he has been suspended from the faculty of giving absolution, can absolve from such sin.

CIC 1331; 1354–7 CIC 976

1466 Priests must make themselves available to penitents like Christ the Good Shepherd looking for the lost sheep, and the Good Samaritan binding up the wounds of sin, welcoming the prodigal son with a judgement that is at the same time just and merciful, since the priest is not the master of God's pardon, but the servant.

CIC 986 PO 13

1467 Every priest must keep totally secret all that he is told by penitents, under pain of excommunication. This is called the *Seal of Confession*, because what is told to the priest remains *sealed* by the sacrament.

CIC 1388

The effects of the Sacrament

1468 'If its root is bitter, its fruit is very sweet'. Those who are reconciled with God in the sacrament of Penance, experience peace and serenity of conscience, joined to a great consolation of soul because they rise again from their sins to rejoice in God's friendship with the sunshine of the soul that it brings. They are also reestablished in the family of the Church rejoicing together with him.

RC 2,5,18 Trent DS 1674 Jn 5,24 RP 31 1 Cor 12,2

The celebration of the Sacrament

1480 Individual and integral confession of sins followed by absolution, remains the ordinary way by which the faithful are reconciled with God and the Church, unless a physical or moral impossibility prevents this. The basic reason for this is that Christ personally addresses himself to each penitent, telling them that their sins are forgiven. This significance is maintained when there is a communal celebration of Penance with individual absolution.

OP 31

Mk 2, 5

1483 General absolution is allowed under strict conditions: danger of death, and vast numbers of

people; but there is a grave obligation in
conscience to confess each mortal sin to a priest   RP 33
subsequently.   CIC 962

Indulgences

1471   Indulgences are prayers or good deeds which the
       Church enriches by the merits of Christ and the
       Communion of Saints to make reparation for our
       sins.

1472   Every sin we commit leaves behind that unhealthy   cf. Heb
       attachment which, if it is not atoned for here on   12,1
       earth, will be purified in Purgatory. We call this
       process the working out of the *temporal*
       punishment due to sin. The Church, which has the   CIC 992
       power of binding and loosing, can draw on the
       merits of Our Lord, Our Lady and the saints to
       remit such punishment either *in part* (partial) or in
       full (plenary) by means of acts of devotion, such
       as the Rosary and the Stations of the Cross;
       adoration of the Blessed Sacrament or devout
       reading of Scripture for at least half an hour (to all
       of *which are attached* plenary indulgences.)*

The Sacrament of the Anointing of the Sick

1499   The Church commends the sick to Christ who
       suffered, died and rose in glory, through the holy
       anointing and the prayer of priests.

                                                        LG 11

The basis for the Sacrament in the economy of salvation

1500   Israel turned to the Lord for mercy and for healing:
       'Have mercy on me, Lord, I have no strength; Lord,
       heal me, my body is racked' (Ps 6, 3). Sickness was
       linked in a mysterious way with sin and the neglect
       of God's Law, but gradually assumed a redemptive   Is 53,11;
       role through the preaching of the prophets.   33,34

1503   For Christ it was not that sickness was to be seen
       as the penalty for sin, but rather 'that the works of

---

*three conditions are necessary : sacramental confession, Holy Communion and
prayer for the Pope's intentions (one Our Father and one Hail Mary.)

God might be made manifest' (Jn 9, 3). In him the healing power of God flows out to cure all who approach him with faith. Moreover he takes upon himself the burden of our infirmities and our sicknesses, as he took upon himself our sins as the Lamb of God.

Mk 1,41;3,1
Lk 6,19
Mt 8,17
Mt 11,4
Jn 1,29

1506 Christ in turn sent his disciples to heal 'and anoint with oil' (Mk 6, 12) in his name and promised that they would lay their hands on the sick who would recover, as a sign that the kingdom of God had come. S. Paul associated such healing with reception of the Eucharist but also saw God's power made perfect in weakness. S. James attests the existence of a special sacrament for the sick: 'Is one of you sick? Let him send for the elders of the church, and let them pray over him, anointing him with oil in the Lord's name; and the prayer of faith will save the sick man, and the Lord will raise him up; and if he has committed any sins, they will be pardoned' (Jas 5, 14–15).

Mt 10,7–8
Mk 16,18
1 Cor 11,30
2 Cor 12,9

The recipient and the minister of the Sacrament

1514 The anointing of the sick is not only for those who are at the point of death, but for all those whose illness or old age begins to put them in that danger. It can be received several times even during the same illness. Only bishops and priests can administer the anointing of the sick.

Trent
DS 1697;
1719
CIC 1003

The celebration of the Sacrament

1517 The liturgy of the word preceded by a rite of penance begins the celebration, which is followed by the imposition of hands in silence and then the prayer which is the *epiclesis*; the forehead and the hands are then anointed with the oil of the sick. If at all possible it should take place within the context of the Eucharist.

The effects of the Sacrament

1520 The first grace of this sacrament is the gift of the Holy Spirit to bring comfort, peace and a certain courage to confront the particular illness or the weakness of old age, and to strengthen the soul against the attack of the devil who conjures up the vision of our sins ' ...and if he has committed any sins, they will be forgiven' (Jas 5,15). It also unites us to the redemptive passion of Our Saviour together with the whole Church which prays in union with Him and finally prepares us for that moment when we leave this life, to go to our Father's house.

Heb 2,15

Trent
DS 1717
Trent
DS 1698
DS 1694

Viaticum

1524 If possible the anointing of the sick is given in the context of the sacraments of Penance, and Holy Eucharist. But if death is imminent, this Holy Communion is called *viaticum*, received for that last journey of the Christian soul, fulfilling Christ's words 'He who eats my flesh and drinks my blood has eternal life, and I will raise him up at the last day' (Jn 6, 54).

Chapter 3: The Sacraments of Consecrated Ministry: Holy Orders and Matrimony

1535 In these two sacraments those who are already consecrated by baptism and confirmation as a kingdom of priests and a holy people can receive a further consecration, as pastors or as spouses.

The Sacrament of Orders

1536 This is the sacrament by which the mission of Christ given to the apostles, is continued in the Church through the ages. It comprises three degrees: the episcopate, the priesthood and the diaconate.

The name 'Order'

1537 *Order* in ancient Rome meant the civil service, or governing body. *Ordination* was therefore incorporation into the Order. In the Christian sense, Ordination is a sacramental act by which a

Heb 5,6;
7,11
Ps 110,4

lay person enters the Order of Bishop, Priest or Deacon and by the gift of the Holy Spirit is able to exercise a sacred power. This does not come from the community, but from Christ through His Church, and is a consecration by the imposition of hands.   LG 10

The Sacrament of Orders in the Old Testament

1539   The Chosen People was that holy nation, a kingdom of priests, called into existence by God. One of the twelve tribes was further set apart to serve in the worship of God and have him as their inheritance. The sons of Aaron were consecrated to serve the tabernacle of the Lord, to preach and to offer sacrifice 'chosen from among men (and) appointed to act on behalf of men in relation to God, to offer gifts and sacrifices for sins' (Heb 5, 1). Moses also chose seventy of the elders who received some of his spirit to bear his burden of office. The Church draws on all these former 'orders' in the Latin rite ritual for Bishop, Priest and Deacon.

Ex 19,6
Is 61,6
Num 1,48–53
Jos 13,33

Num 11,16f

The unique priesthood of Christ

1544   The priesthood of the Old Testament was not able to offer that perfect sacrifice of praise and expiation until Christ, Great High Priest of the order of Melchisedech, once more took into his holy and immaculate hands the gifts of bread and wine and by 'a single offering has perfected for all time those whom he sanctifies' (Heb 10,14). He is the unique and perfect priest, 'the one mediator between God and men' (I Tim 2,5), who acts in his priests and makes his people a kingdom of priests. Although the ministerial priesthood is at the service of the baptised people of God, it alone provides the means by which Christ builds up and guides his Church through their ordination.

Rev 5,9–10
LG 10

In persona Christi capitis (In the person of Christ the head)

1548   Christ, the head of the Church, shepherd of his flock, high priest and teacher of truth, is present

LG 10.28

in his Church through the person of the ordained
minister who acts *in persona Christi*. This means
that even sin cannot prevent the grace of Christ
from bearing fruit in those who receive the sacraments from him, but of course personal infidelity
will damage the impact of that grace.

1551 The priesthood is *ministerial*, a priesthood which
serves Christ in his members. It is not given for
personal honour, but to look after the flock of LG 24
Christ out of love for the Good Shepherd Himself. 1 Pt 5,3

In the name of the whole Church

1552 The priest is not elected or delegated by the people
but is Christ's representative. By the very fact of
offering the prayer and sacrifice of Christ the
Head, he also offers the worship of all the
members. The whole Church prays 'through Him,
with Him and in Him in the unity of the Holy
Spirit to the glory of God the Father'.

The Three Degrees of the Sacrament of Orders

1554 Catholic doctrine recognises two degrees of
participation in the ministerial priesthood of
Christ: the episcopate and the priesthood; and a
third degree of *service*, the diaconate, which
together make up the Sacrament of Orders. LG 28

1555 *The Bishop* receives the *fulness* of the sacrament LG 21
of Orders. His consecration sanctifies him as well
as giving him the office of teaching and ruling his
diocese.* He also becomes a member of the LG 22
college of bishops, an expression of which is given
by the presence of several bishops who take part in
consecration at the laying on of hands. The unity
between all the bishops is provided by the Bishop
of Rome, without whose intervention no consecration takes place. CIC 377

1562 *Priests* are cooperators with the Bishop and share PO 2
in his priesthood to a subordinate degree. They do

---

*Even bishops who have no 'ordinary' jurisdiction, such as *auxiliary* bishops are
given a 'nominal' diocese which once possessed its own bishop.

not have that fulness of the episcopal office, but
they are true priests, consecrated to preach the   LG 28
Gospel, in its widest meaning, and to offer the   OT 20
sacrifice of Christ in the Eucharist. Their promise
of obedience at ordination, as well as the kiss of
peace, signifies their union and communion with
the bishop; while the fact that all priests present at
an ordination impose their hands reveals that all
of them belong to the one *presbyterium*, or college
of priests united with their bishop.   PO 8

The Ordination of Deacons

1569   When he ordains a deacon, only the bishop
imposes his hands, to signify that the deacon is
linked with him in his *diakonía* or ministry, but
does not share in the priesthood.

1570   He does receive through Holy Orders the *seal* or
character which in his case shapes him to Christ,   Mk 10,4
the *servant* of all. Deacons assist the bishop and   Lk 22,2
the priest in the liturgy by distributing Holy
Communion, proclaiming the Gospel and preaching the homily, celebrating the Sacrament of
baptism, assisting at marriages and blessing them,
presiding at funerals and engaging in various
works of charity.   LG 29

1571   The *Permanent Diaconate* (which can be confered
on married men) has since Vatican II become
established in many countries.   LG 29

The celebration of the Sacrament

1572   Each ordination should preferably take place on a
Sunday or holy day in the cathedral so that its
importance can be underlined and people can
attend in large numbers. The imposition of hands,
common to all three degrees of Holy Orders, takes
place during the Eucharist.

1574   The particular character of each Order is brought
out by additional rites. Both the bishop and the
priest are anointed with chrism, to signify their
consecration as priests; the bishop receives the

ring, mitre, crosier and book of the Gospels to mark him as wedded to his diocese and the flock of which he is the shepherd, and as an upholder of the faith of the Church. The priest receives the chalice and paten, symbol of the sacrifice which he is to offer for the people. The deacon, because he is charged to proclaim the word of God receives the book of the Gospels.

The minister

1575   Christ continues to call some to be apostles, and   Eph 4,11
others to be pastors, through bishops who them-
selves have been validly ordained. They alone can
confer the three degrees of Holy Orders.

The recipient

1578   Nobody has the right to receive Holy Orders; 'he
is called by God, just as Aaron was' (Heb 5,4).
The Church recognises that the restriction of the   CIC 1024
priesthood to men is willed by Christ in his choice   MD 26–7
of men to be apostles, and sanctioned by the
constant Tradition of the Church.

1577   The Church also normally only calls those men
who have freely chosen celibacy 'for the kingdom   1 Cor 7,32
of heaven' (Mt 19,12). Celibacy is an expression of   PO 16
the gift of oneself to God and the Church out of   PV 50
generous love.   VS 22

The effects of the Sacrament

1581   As with Baptism and Confirmation, so does Holy
Orders give a share in Christ's own office which
cannot be removed because it confers a permanent
character.

1583   Those priests who are returned to the lay state do   DS 1774
not in fact become laymen, because the character   CIC 290–3
of the priesthood remains and they are called to
exercise their power of absolution when they come
across someone in danger of death, but they cease
to practise as priests, or are forbidden to do so.

1586   The bishop by ordination is given the strength to
lead his church as father and shepherd, feeding

them with truth and love. The priest also through Baptism and the Eucharist sees his own flock grow in faith and model themselves on Christ, while the deacon is given the grace to serve the people in his 'ministry'.   LG 29

The Sacrament of Matrimony

1601   The covenant of marriage by which a man and a woman begin a mutual partnership for the whole of their lives, is by its very character ordained to the good of the spouses themselves as well as the procreation and education of their children and has been raised by Christ to the dignity of a sacrament.   CIC 1055

Matrimony in God's Plan

1602   The vocation of marriage is woven into the very nature of man and woman. It is not simply a   GS 48
human institution but written into the very design of creation by God which is never totally obscured by man's hardness of heart. God who is Love itself created man and woman in his image, and made their love for each other an image of that undying love with which he loves mankind. As that love is fruitful, so God blessed their love telling them, 'Be fruitful and multiply, and fill the earth and subdue it' (Gen 1,28). Moreover man and woman are created for each other so that they   Gen 2,18
can become one flesh.   Mt 19,6

Matrimony 'under the law of sin'   Rom 7,7

1606   Our faith tells us that deep internal disorders are due to sin, not, in the case of married people, due to their nature as man and wife nor to their relationship. As a result of original sin, there is now in their relationship a craving and a wish to   Gen 3,16
dominate; and child-bearing and subduing the   Gen 3,16.18
earth are overlaid with pain and resentment. God   Gen 3,21
has always, from the beginning, come to assist with his grace, so that selfishness may be overcome. He aims to protect women from arbitrary domination by man through the Law

given to Moses, and through the prophets outlines that faithful and indissoluble covenant, 'strong as death', and holds up the examples of Tobias and Ruth.

Jesus' teaching about Matrimony

1612   The Church puts great store by Jesus' first miracle at the marriage feast of Cana, for in it she sees a confirmation of the goodness of marriage as an institution which will be a sign of Christ's presence.   Jn 2,1–11

1615   Jesus preached the indissoluble union of man and wife as having been intended in the beginning by the Creator, rejecting the divorce as granted by Moses because of 'hardness of heart', which 'from the beginning was not so' (Mt 19,8). Christ at the same time provides the grace to live according to that original standard, making his Cross the strength of the spouses, enabling them to surrender their selfishness: 'Husbands, love your wives, as Christ loved the Church and gave himself up for her' (Eph 5,25–26). Marriage is the sacrament of Christ's covenant with the Church, which looks towards that vision of the marriage of the Lamb.   Rev 19,7.9

Virginity for the sake of the kingdom

1618   The Lord gives the grace both to live the married   FC 16
life and that great vocation of virginity for the sake of the kingdom. Those who accept virginity 'to follow the Lamb wherever he goes' (Rev 14,4), are a reminder that even the mystery of marriage   Mt 19,12
will one day pass away and the Bridegroom will   Mk 12,24f
return.   Mt 25,1–14

The celebration of Matrimony

1621   In the Latin rite the ceremony normally takes place during the Eucharist, so that the spouses can offer themselves to each other and seal that offering in Christ's own sacrifice and Communion.

1623 In the Latin rite the spouses are considered to be the ministers of matrimony, whereas in the oriental liturgies the minister is the bishop or priest, who receives their vows and puts a crown on each. Hence the rite of Matrimony is called *The Office of Crowning* (*Akolouthia tou stephanōmatos*).

Matrimonial consent

1625 The Church considers the exchange of consent as the essential element of matrimony; without it, there is no marriage.

CIC 1057

1627 The consent must be given without any reservation, free from any legal or ecclesiastical constraint and without any outside pressure, usually described as 'force or fear'.

GS 48
CIC 1103

1630 The priest or deacon receives this consent in the name of the Church and gives the Church's blessing, signifying that this is truly a sacrament of the Church.

1632 Marriage preparation is of first importance and should emphasise the dignity of married love and the place of chastity in marriage, so that couples can be prepared to live it in their marriage.

Mixed marriages and those of disparity of cult

1633 A mixed marriage is between a Catholic and a baptised non Catholic.
A marriage with disparity of cult is between a Catholic and a non-Christian.

1634 The difficulties of mixed marriages must not be underestimated, because there is a risk that the drama of Christian disunity can be played out in the family. This is even graver when we consider marriages with disparity of cult. There is a problem about the difference of religion and diverse religious mentalities, and the question of the education of children as well as the Catholic Church's teaching on moral questions connected with marriage.

1635   In the Latin rite a mixed marriage needs an express *permission* for *licitness* from the ecclesiastical authorities; in cases of disparity of cult, a *dispensation* is needed *for validity*. Both the permission and the dispensation include the obligation undertaken by the Catholic party to baptise and educate all children born of the marriage in the Catholic faith.   CIC 1124   CIC 1086   CIC 1125

The effects of Matrimony

1639   God provides a seal to marriage which is called the marriage bond which once concluded and consummated, cannot be dissolved.   CIC 1141

1640   The Church can declare the *nullity* of a marriage after examination by an ecclesiastical tribunal. This states that the marriage never in fact existed and the contracting parties are free to contract a valid marriage with another partner.

1641   Christ gives a special grace to spouses to perfect their love and deepen their unity, so that they can sanctify themselves and be prepared for the duties of family life.

The unity and indissolubility of Matrimony and the fidelity of married love

1643   Husband and wife in marriage are no longer two, but become one flesh. They are called to grow continually in their communion through day-to-day fidelity to their marriage promise of total mutual self-giving. Polygamy and polyandry run counter to such a promise.   FC 19

1646   God loves us with an undivided love and gives spouses a share in that love, which sustains them and helps them in their fidelity to bear witness to the faithful love of God. Those who remain faithful in often heroic conditions should be honoured and supported by the church community.

1649   When the situation becomes impossible a physical *separation* can be envisaged − but not a divorce, because the couple remain married. The

Church cannot recognise a second union when the first one remains valid. Those who remarry civilly break the law of God and are forbidden to go to Communion. They can only be readmitted to the sacraments if they agree to live in perfect continence. FC 83 Mk 10, 11–12

Openness to life

1652 The institution of marriage and married love are of their nature ordained to the procreation and education of children and find in them their crown. GS 48

1653 Parents are not only called to bring children into the world, but to be the ministers to them of the knowledge and love of God. The family is the 'domestic Church' in which the parents are the first preachers of the faith and should be the first prompters of that love. They should take into consideration the possibility of a child's religious vocation as the fulfilment of their shared love and faith. LG 11

Sacramentals

1667 Sacramentals do not confer grace in the same way as sacraments, but through the prayer of the Church prepare people to receive grace and dispose them to cooperate with it.

1668 They are instituted by the Church to sanctify various ministries or states of life in the Church, or articles of devotion. There is always a prayer, usually accompanied by a sign, such as the imposition of a hand, the sign of the Cross or a blessing.

1671 Various *blessings* consecrate persons or objects to God: the blessing of an abbot or abbess, the consecration of virgins, the rite of religious profession, the blessing of lectors, acolytes and catechists, the dedication of a Church or an altar, the blessing of the holy oils, of a chalice and paten, of vestments and of Church bells and of holy water. *Exorcism* in its strict sense (an Eph 1,3 exorcism is part of Baptism) is only carried out by a priest with permission of the bishop; before proceeding one has to be sure it is a question of the presence of the Devil or evil spirits, and not some other cause.   CIC 1172

Christian funerals

1680   All the sacraments look towards that last Passover which allows the Christian to enter through the doors of death into the life of the kingdom of heaven.

The last passover of the Christian

1681   The Christian understanding of death can only be seen in the light of the mystery of Christ's death, resurrection and ascension. It is because of this that we can look forward to leaving this body and dwelling with the Lord. Death is the final   2 Cor 5,8
fulfilment of that new life begun in Baptism and completed in Confirmation, which looks to the heavenly banquet already anticipated in the Eucharist, when what remains is the wedding garment after the purification of Purgatory.

The celebration of funerals

1684   The *Order of Funeral Rites* of the Roman liturgy envisages three types of celebration which correspond to the three places where these take place: the house of the deceased, the Church, and the cemetery (or crematorium). Each celebration has four stages:
   a) *The welcome of the community* which allows   I Thes 4,18
   those words of consolation to be directed to the grieving relatives and to bring to the attention of the community the death of one of their number.
   b) *The liturgy of the word* which should not be a panegyric.
   c) *The Eucharistic Sacrifice* in which the Church asks that the deceased may be granted pardon for sin and admission to heaven.
   d) *The farewell* or *commendation*, before the body which was reborn in Christ goes to its last resting-place.

Part Three:
Life in Christ

1691 'Christian, know your dignity; because now you share in the divine nature do not return to your old baseness by degenerate conduct. Remember the Head and the Body to which you belong. Recall that you have been snatched from the power of darkness and brought into the light and into God's Kingdom.'   Leo I
                                                                                    Serm 21,2

Life in the Spirit – The Human Vocation

Chapter 1: The Dignity of the Human Person

Man, made in the Image of God

1700 The divine image is present in every individual human being. It shines out also in the union of two persons in one flesh, which is an image of the union of the divine Persons in the Trinity.

1702 Each individual because he possesses an immortal spiritual soul, is willed into existence directly by God and destined for eternal happiness. By reason man can see the order of God in creation and because he has free will he can seek the truth in love.   GS 14

GS 24

GS 15

1706 The voice of God, which is the law that man hears in his conscience, tells him to avoid evil and do good. The whole dignity of man rests on that moral law. At the beginning of history, man abused his liberty, was seduced by the devil and succumbed to temptation and sin.   GS 16

GS 13

1708 By his passion Christ delivered us from the devil and from sin, and won for us that grace of adoption which in union with him leads to sanctity.

We are called to happiness

1716 The beatitudes (Mt 5, 3 – 12) describe the actions and dispositions that should characterise the Christian life. They also proclaim the reward already won by Christ's disciples in the life of Our Lady and the saints, and to some extent in the lives of all those who are faithful.   VS 16

1720 The New Testament uses several expressions to explain the nature of the Christian notion of happiness: the coming of God's kingdom, the Mt 4,17

vision of God, entry into the joy of the Lord, entry
into God's rest. Yet what is in fact a call to share   Mt 5,8
in the very life of the Trinity is beyond human   Mt 25,21.23
powers, and demands the supernatural gift of   Heb 4,7–11
God's grace.   2 Pt 1,4

1723   This places us in the realm of moral choice, for if   VS 18
true happiness lies in keeping the commandments,
accepting the teaching of Christ and that of the
Church, we have to renounce all that stands in the
way.

Human freedom

1731   Freedom is that power which is rooted in the
reason and the will, to act or refrain from acting   Sir 15,14
by deliberate choice; but in the context of the final
end of man, it is the choice between good and evil.

1732   The pursuit of good makes man truly free, while   VS 34
the choice of evil leads to the abuse of liberty and   Rom 6,17
the slavery of sin. We are responsible for our
freely chosen decisions; our freedom, and hence   Ez 18,1f
our responsibility, can be diminished by ignor-   Gen 4,10
ance, inadvertence, or pressure from force or fear,   2 Sam
and by our habits and passions. Everyone's   12,7–15
freedom has the right to be respected within the
limits of the common good and the interests of
public order.   DH 7

1739   Christ has obtained for us the glorious liberty of
the sons of God by his Cross, and given us his   Rom 8,21
Spirit: 'for where the Spirit of the Lord is, there is
freedom' (2 Cor 3, 17). The grace of God does not
pose a threat to our freedom, because it prompts
us to respond to the truth in love which makes us
truly free.

The Morality of Human Acts

1750   The morality of human acts depends on the
object, together with the intention and circumstances.

1753   A morally good act presupposes that the object, intention and circumstances are all good. An evil intention undermines the goodness of the act ('fasting to be seen by men'). A good motive cannot mitigate an essentially evil act.

Mt 6,1
RP 17
VS 81

1755   It is quite wrong to judge the morality of human acts without taking into consideration *all* the elements which go to make them up and we should bear in mind that it is never permitted to do evil that good may come out of it.

Rom 3,8

The Morality of Human Emotions

1763   The passions, feelings, emotions which make up the human psyche are in themselves neither morally good nor evil. They become morally good when they come under the command or assent of the mind and will − that is, when they become involved in a human act. Moral perfection involves the *whole* person, *'my heart and flesh sing for joy to the living God'* (Ps 84,3).

Aquinas
ST 1−2 24,1
2−2 24,3

Moral conscience

1777   'In the depths of his conscience man discovers the presence of a law which he did not give to himself but which he must obey . . . to love and fulfil what is right and to avoid what is evil . . . The conscience is . . . that sanctuary where one is alone with God and where his voice is heard'.

GS 16

1778   The moral conscience is a judgement made by the mind by which a person takes stock of the morality of an action which he is contemplating and is about to carry out. Both interior reflection and prudence are necessary for a correct conscience. Man must not be made to act against his conscience, and at the same time must not be prevented from following it, for as Cardinal Newman says 'Conscience has rights because it has duties'. It must be correctly formed, and such formation takes a whole lifetime. The education of children should prudently include instruction

DH 3
Newman
Diff 2
p. 250

VS 34

on virtue: it should deal with fear, egoism, pride, the feelings of guilt and the feelings of pleasure which come from weakness and human sin. The word of God should always be a light on our path which helps us in our examination of conscience.   Ps 119,109
We are also assisted by the gifts of the Holy Spirit,   DH 14
the good advice of others and the authoritative teaching of the Church.

1783   'Our aim', says the Letter to Timothy, is 'love that issues from a pure heart and a good conscience and sincere faith' (1 Tim 1, 5). However it can happen that the conscience misleads. This may be   GS 16
due to gradual blindness which has been allowed to obscure the difference between good and evil. If one has knowingly and freely followed bad example, ignored the Gospel, given way to sensuality, rejected the known truth in teachings of the Church, then one is guilty. But if for example the ignorance is invincible then there is no guilt even though there is disorder and evil present which needs correction.   VS 62

The Virtues

1803   'All that rings true, all that commands reverence, and all that makes for right; all that is pure, all that is lovely, all that is gracious in the telling; virtue and merit, whenever virtue and merit are found — let this be the argument of your thoughts'. (Phil 4, 8).

1804   The human virtues are those habitual dispositions of the mind and will which regulate our actions, rule our passions and guide our conduct so that we can live a morally good life. *Moral* virtues are acquired by us, whereas *theological* virtues are infused in us by God.

1805   The four *cardinal* (because all others *hinge* on them) *moral* virtues are prudence (to see the good and choose it); justice (to give God and our neighbour their due); courage (the strength to persevere) and temperance (which controls the passions and creates a sense of balance).

1810   Given the effects of sin and our natural weakness, human moral virtues, which are acquired by education and by persevering in good, need the help of divine grace. We must ask God for this and make use of the sacraments.

1812   The *theological virtues* are infused by God into the soul, so that we can become capable of acting as children of God. They are also the pledge of the presence and action of the Holy Spirit within us. *Faith* is a gift of God, that virtue by which we believe in God and all that he has said and revealed   DV 5
because he is truth itself. The disciple of Christ must not only keep faith with God, but must also bear witness to it. *Hope* is that virtue by which we   Mt 10,
desire the kingdom of heaven and eternal life,   32–33
putting our confidence in the promises of Christ and relying not on our own strength but on the grace of the Holy Spirit. Hope finds its model in Abraham, who 'hoping against hope, (he) believed and became the father of many nations' (Rom 4,18). *Charity* is that virtue by which we love God above all things for his sake, and love our neighbour as ourselves for love of God. Jesus made charity his new commandment. It is the   Jn 15,12
greatest of the virtues and the source of all   1 Cor 13,13
Christian life, which allows us to respond to 'Him who first loved us' (1 Jn 4,19). The fruits of charity are joy, peace and mercy.

1830   *The gifts of the Holy Spirit* are wisdom, understanding, counsel, fortitude, knowledge, piety and the fear of the Lord. They perfect the virtues in those who receive them and make them responsive to God's inspirations. *The fruits of the Holy Spirit* are love, joy, peace, patience*, kindness, generosity, forbearance, gentleness, faithfulness,   Gal
courtesy*, temperateness* and self control.   5,22–23

Sin

1849   Sin has been defined by S. Augustine as 'a word,   Faust, 22,27
an action or a desire contrary to the divine law'.

---

* These are not found in the Greek text. It is possible that two renderings of the same word have been accidentally included.

Sin from the first has been an act of revolt against God: 'love of self even to the point of contempt for God'. At the hour when sin seemed to triumph, the Cross was planted to bring the greatest pardon.

Aug
civ Dei
14,28

Jn 14,30

1852 Sin can be listed according to object or opposing virtue, or alongside each commandment; it can be spiritual or carnal, or again in thought, word, deed or by omission. Above all it can be *mortal* or *venial*.

VS 70

1855 *Mortal sin* destroys charity in the heart of man by a grave violation of the law of God. For this there must be grave matter (against the commandments) and there must be full knowledge and free deliberate consent. *Venial* sin, because it lacks one or more of these components, does not deprive us of that love of God and his sanctifying grace, but it does lead us to commit sin unless we repent of it.

1868 We can also cooperate in sin either directly or by command, counsel, praise or approval, by concealment, silence, or by defending the ill done.

1866 *Capital sins* which generate other vices are pride, avarice, envy, anger, impurity, gluttony and sloth.

1867 The *sins crying to heaven for vengeance* are wilful murder, the sin of the Sodomites, oppression of the poor, the plea of the stranger, the widow and the orphan and those unjustly defrauded of their wages.

Gen 4,10
Gen 18,20
Ex 3,7–10
Ex 22,20–22
Jas 5,4

Chapter 2: The Human Community

The communitarian dimension of the human vocation

1879 *Society* or community is a grouping of people drawn together in an organic way by a principle of unity which is greater than any individual. Certain societies like the family and the city are natural to man; other groupings whether for professional, sporting or political reasons help to bring individuals into a great participation to their own benefit, as well as to the benefit of the group as a whole. But such *socialisation* if pushed too far, can stifle the individual, and hence the principle of *subsidiarity* which sets down as a tenet that 'a society on a higher level should not interfere in the internal life of a society on a lower level' and that CA 48 decisions should therefore be always devolved to the lowest appropriate level. This obviously has implications on the shop-floor, but can also be applied to national and regional interests, and in the field of international relations.

Sharing in society

1897 Every community has need of an *authority* to govern it and this authority emanates ultimately Leo XIII from God, as Christ remarked to Pilate, 'You Immortale would have no power over me unless it had been Dei. DS 316 given you from above' (Jn 19,11). The authority Rom in a State is entitled to honour and obedience but 13,1−2 in its turn it must use morally licit means and act 1 Pt 2,13f for the common good. GS 74

1905 The *common good* is the sum of social conditions which all groups and their individual members need to reach their ultimate fulfilment. This has a GS 26 social and a personal dimension and requires a stable and secure basis in which each person can GS 84 take the fulness of his human civic responsibilities seriously. GS 31

Social justice

1929 Social justice is the link between the exercise of authority and the common good. It demands that Pius XI any legislation should safeguard the rights of the QA 57 individual by respecting the dignity of each and Mt 25, their diverse talents, while striving to redress the 14−30 inequalities in society. This of itself argues that we GS 29 become aware of our interdependence (*solidarity*) SRS 38−40 as much on the level of management and workers as between nation and nation, rich and poor; for 'as you did it to one of the least of these my brethren, you did it to me' (Mt 25,40).

Chapter 3: Law and Grace, the working of God's salvation

The moral law

1950   'The Law has found its fulfilment in Christ, that everyone who has faith will be justified' (Rom 10,4). This is because He is that Incarnate Wisdom who in his life and actions is the way that is true righteousness and leads to holiness.

The natural moral law

1954   The Natural Moral Law allows man to discern with his reason the difference between good and evil, truth and falsehood. It is nothing less than VS 19
the light of our mind by which God allows us to   Aquinas
see what should be done and what should be   Dec prae
avoided. It is for all mankind and does not vary   GS 10
and thus is a firm foundation for civil law and for public morality. But the precepts of natural law are not self-evident to fallen man, and need the help of grace to be clearly developed.

The law given to Israel

1961   The Law given to Israel which is summarised in the Ten Commandments worked as a light to man's conscience showing the ways of God which lead to life and the ways of evil. 'God wrote on the   Dt 30,15
tables of the Law what men did not read in their   Ps 57,1
hearts' says S. Augustine. Although holy and   Rom 7,12f
good, the old law remained imperfect, because, due to sin man was incapable of keeping it: S. Paul says that its primary purpose was to highlight the presence of concupiscence in the heart of man.   VS 45

The new law of the Gospel

1965   The Law comes to its perfection in Christ with the Sermon on the Mount, but it is also the work of the Holy Spirit writing his Law in the hearts of   Jer 31,3
believers, so that the Lord will be their God and   Heb 8,8–11
they will be His people. It is summarised in the

words of Our Lord: 'Whatever you wish that men would do to you, do so to them, for this is the Law and the Prophets' (Mt 7,12), and in His new commandment to love one another as He has loved us.

Lk 6,31
Jn 15,12

Grace and justification

1987   The first work of the grace of the Holy Spirit is that conversion of heart which detaches man from sin and brings us faith, hope, charity and acceptance of God's will. This state of *justification* is won for us by the passion of Christ and is a work of the love of God in us through the Holy Spirit.

Mt 4,17

Rom 3,21

1996   *Grace* is a share in the life of God, which being supernatural is a totally free gift which prompts us even to accept it. It can be *sanctifying* (i.e. Baptismal grace) or *habitual*, or *actual* or *sacramental* or a *grace of state* (i.e. priesthood).

2006   *Merit* flows from the fact that God has freely chosen to associate mankind in the work of his grace; our merit as sons of God comes from our adoption by him. The love of God which is the source of all merit is also the source of all sanctity: the final reward of goodness.

Trent
DS 1546
1548

LG 40
Trent
DS 1576

The Church Mother and Teacher

Moral life and the magisterium of the Church

2032   The Church has received from the apostles the commandment of Christ to preach the saving truths of the Gospel. It is because of this that it belongs to her 'always and everywhere to announce moral principles, including those pertaining to the social order, and to make judgements on human affairs to the extent that they are required by the fundamental rights of the human person or the salvation of souls'.

CIC 747

2033   Normally the Magisterium of the Church is exercised in preaching or in catechetical instruction, with the help of theologians and spiritual writers. Such teaching will include *the Creed, the Our Father* and *the Ten Commandments*

2034   In addition the Roman pontiff and the bishops teach the people the faith and its application to human morality through their ordinary Magisterium. It is not simply matters of doctrine which are covered by the charism of infallibility but also the moral applications without which the saving truths of the faith 'cannot be rightly preserved and expounded'. The authority of the Magisterium also extends to specific precepts of the natural law on the same principle.

LG 25

VS 37

ME 3

2038   The Church needs the devotion of its pastors, the intellectual skills of its theologians and the good will of the faithful, so that the faith can be applied in all situations. However, in making individual judgements, the danger of setting one's own conscience against the moral law or the Magisterium must be avoided, because one risks separating oneself from that communion that is the flock of Christ.

VS 111

The Commandments of the Church

2041   These are obligatory for the faithful because they are the indispensable minimum demanded for the practice of the faith.
   1. To keep the Sundays holy in honour of Our Lord's resurrection by taking part in the Eucharist. This also applies to Holidays of Obligation.

CIC 1246 – 8

   2. To go to the Sacrament of Penance at least once a year.

CIC 989

   3. To receive Holy Communion at least once a year, during Paschal time. This lays down a basic minimal observance. A Christian must at least take part in the celebration of the Resurrection which is the central feast of the Church's year.

CIC 1249-51

   4. To observe the prescriptions relating to fasting and abstinence. [In USA all Fridays in Lent are days on which no meat should be eaten; this does not apply to Britain. Ash Wednesday and Good Friday are days of fasting and abstinence from meat in both countries.]

5. To contribute to the Church's needs so that she   CIC 222
   can provide what is necessary for divine
   worship, can support the clergy and engage in
   apostolic works of charity.   CIC 920

Section II: The Ten Commandments

Exodus 20, 2–17

I am the Lord your God, who brought you out of the land of Egypt, out of the house of bondage.
You shall have no other gods before me.

You shall not make for yourself a graven image, or any likeness of anything that is in heaven above, or that is in the earth beneath, or that is in the water under the earth; you shall not bow down to them or serve them; for I the Lord your God am a jealous God, visiting the iniquity of the fathers upon the children of the third and fourth generation of those who hate me, but showing steadfast love to thousands of those who love me and keep my commandments.
You shall not take the name of the Lord your God in vain; for the Lord will not hold him guiltless who takes his name in vain.

Remember the sabbath day, to keep it holy. Six days you shall labour, and do all your work; but the seventh day is a sabbath to the Lord your God; in it you shall not do any work, you, or your son, or your daughter, your manservant, or your maidservant, or your cattle, or the sojourner who is within your gates; for in six days the Lord made heaven and earth, the sea, and all that is in them, and rested the seventh day; therefore the Lord blessed the sabbath day and hallowed it.

Deuteronomy 5, 6–21

I am the Lord your God, who brought you out of the land of Egypt, out of the house of bondage.
You shall have no other gods before me.

You shall not make for yourself a graven image, or any likeness of anything that is in heaven above, or that is on the earth beneath, or that is in the water under the earth; you shall not bow down to them or serve them; for I the Lord your God am a jealous God, visiting the iniquity of the fathers upon the children to the third and fourth generation of those who hate me, but showing steadfast love to thousands of those who love me and keep my commandments.
You shall not take the name of the Lord your God in vain: for the Lord will not hold him guiltless who takes his name in vain.

Observe the sabbath day, to keep it holy, as the Lord your God commanded you. Six days you shall labour, and do all your work; but the seventh day is a sabbath to the Lord your God; in it you shall not do any work, you, or your son, or your daughter, or your manservant, or your maidservant, or your ox, or your ass, or any of your cattle, or the sojourner who is within your gates, that your manservant and your maidservant may rest as well as you. You shall remember that you were a servant in the land of Egypt, and the Lord your God brought you out thence with a mighty hand and an outstretched arm; therefore the Lord your God commanded you to keep the sabbath day.

1
I am the Lord your God.

You shall have no other gods before me.

2
You shall not take the name of the Lord your God in vain.

3
Remember to keep holy the sabbath day.

120

Honour your father and your mother, that your days may be long in the land which the Lord your God gives you.	Honour your father and your mother, as the Lord your God commanded you; that your days may be prolonged, and that it may go well with you in the land which the Lord your God gives you.	4 Honour your father and your mother.
You shall not kill.	You shall not kill.	5 You shall not kill.
You shall not commit adultery	Neither shall you commit adultery.	6 You shall not commit adultery.
You shall not steal.	Neither shall you steal.	7 You shall not steal.
You shall not bear false witness against your neighbour.	Neither shall you bear false witness against your neighbour.	8 You shall not bear false witness.
You shall not covet your neighbour's house; you shall not covet your neighbour's wife, or his manservant, or his maidservant, or his ox, or his ass, or anything that is your neighbour's.	Neither shall you covet your neighbour's wife; and you shall not desire your neighbour's house, his field, or his manservant, or his maidservant, his ox or his ass, or anything that is your neighbour's.	9 You shall not covet your neighbour's wife 10 You shall not covet your neighbour's goods.

II The Ten Commandments

2052 'If you would be perfect', said Jesus in reply to the rich young man, 'Go, sell what you have and give to the poor, and you will have treasure in heaven; and come, follow me' (Mt 19,21).

2054 Jesus did not come to abolish the commandments, but to fulfil them at their deepest level, in a way which surpassed the fidelity of the scribes and pharisees; this fulfilment is expressed in the Mt 5,20 commandment to love God and one's neighbour: 'Owe no one anything, except to love one another; for he who loves his neighbour has fulfilled the law. The commandments, "You shall not commit adultery, You shall not kill, You shall not steal, You shall not covet," and any other commandment, are summed up in this sentence, "You shall love your neighbour as yourself". Love does no wrong to a neighbour; therefore love is the fulfilling of the law' (Rom 13,8–11).

The Ten Commandments or Decalogue in Holy Scripture

2056 The Ten Commandments must first be seen against the background of the Exodus, pointing out the path of life after the years of slavery: 'If you obey the commandments of the Lord your God which I command this day, by loving the Lord your God, by walking in his ways, and by keeping his commandments and his statutes and his ordinances, then you shall live and multiply, and the Lord will bless you in the land which you are entering to possess it' (Dt 30,16).

2060 The Ten Commandments which are to be found in Ex 20,1 – 17
the books of Exodus and Deuteronomy are not the Dt 5,6 – 22
precepts of Moses, but the very law of God, written 'with the finger of God' (Ex 31,18) and part of the revelation given to Israel: 'These words the Lord spoke to all your assembly at the mountain out of the midst of the fire, the cloud and the thick darkness, with a loud voice. He added nothing, but wrote them upon two tables of stone, and gave them to me' (Dt 5,22). These Ex 31,18
tablets of stone called the tablets of 'witness' are 32,15

the clauses of the covenant sealed between God and his people: 'and all the people answered with one voice and said, 'All the words which the Lord has spoken we will do' (Ex 24,3).

The Ten Commandments in the Church's Tradition

2065 The Ten Commandments were part of the instruction for catechumens by the fourth century at least and found a place in Church Catechisms by the fifteenth. The division and numbering varies slightly in the Churches of the East.

2067 The Church groups the first three commandments under the love of God and the remaining seven under love of neighbour. All are binding on Christians on pain of sin because they are engraved by God on the heart of man, and conform to his very nature. They are for that reason expressions of natural law, which the Church and revelation make clear for us in the fallen condition of our humanity.

2069 All the Commandments are interlinked, and one cannot break one without infringing the others. We cannot adore and love God without loving our neighbour, which is Jesus' new commandment 'that you love one another as I have loved you' (Jn 15,12). 'These two commandments, on which depend all the Law and the Prophets' (Mt 22,40), are profoundly connected and mutually related. *Their inseparable unity* is attested to by Christ in his words and by his very life: his mission culminates in the Cross of our Redemption (cf. Jn 3,14–15), the sign of his indivisible love for the Father and for humanity (cf Jn 13,1).'   VS 14

Chapter 1: 'You shall love the Lord your God with all your heart, and with all your soul, and with all your mind (Mt 22,37).

First Commandment: *'You will worship the Lord, your God and you will serve Him'.*

2084 It is because God is always the same, faithful and just, the Lord, that we, since we are made in His image, must accept Him totally, put our trust in Him and love Him with all our heart.   Lev 18;19. RC 3,2,4

2086   We must *believe* in Him and all that he reveals. We sin against faith by deliberate doubt which refuses to accept what is part of faith. This refusal is linked to incredulity, which suspends judgement deliberately; both can lead to that blindness which afflicted some of the Pharisees: 'If you were blind, you would have no guilt; but now that you say, "We see" your guilt remains' (Jn 9,41). *Heresy* is the sin committed by a Christian who obstinately denies or openly expresses doubt about a matter of divine and Catholic faith; *apostasy* is the total rejection of the faith; and *schism* is the refusal of submission to the Roman Pontiff or of communion with the members of the Church subject to him.

Rom 1,5; 16,26

CIC 751

2090   *Hope* is not only the expectation that God will fulfil all his promises, but also the fear of offending such eternal love. One offends against hope by *despair*. One also offends by *presumption*, either trusting in one's own efforts or relying on God's mercy without exerting oneself. We are called to love God above all else. We sin against love by *indifference*, *ingratitude*, *lukewarmness* or *spiritual sloth* (accidie). But worst of all we can through pride come to *hate* God and turn against him.

Dt 6,4–5

'You will worship Him alone'

2096   *Adoration* frees us from concentration on ourselves (which is at the root of most sin), so that like Mary we can rejoice in God our Saviour. We express such worship in *prayer* above all, which is the raising of the mind and heart to God in love. We cannot keep the commandments without the spirit of prayer; indeed Our Lord said that we should pray always and not lose heart.

Lk 1,47

Lk 18,1

2099   We must also make of our lives a perfect *sacrifice* to God. Sacrifice, says S. Augustine, is every act of love and worship by which we enter into communion with God and honour Him as Lord of all. It is expressed in that humble and contrite heart that seeks to imitate the Heart of Jesus, pierced for love of us in his perfect sacrifice.

civ Dei 10,6

Ps 51,19

Promises and vows

2101 We make promises to God in Baptism, Confirmation, Matrimony and Holy Orders especially, but we can also promise God certain things out of devotion. If we make a *vow* it is a deliberate and free promise which binds us depending on the degree of seriousness: private, public, simple or solemn. The Church has the power to dispense from vows for certain just causes.

CIC 1191

CIC 692; 1196–7

Religious liberty

2104 The duty of worshipping God is not an individual matter, but also has a social dimension which obliges Christians to make known the one true religion which subsists in the Catholic Church. At the same time this obliges the State to recognise the natural right of individuals to worship God, provided always that it does not go against the common good.

DH 1

DH 7

'You shall have no other gods before me'

2111 *Superstition* attributes an almost magical importance to actions or things themselves, giving them the worship properly due to God alone. *Idolatry* is that divinisation of what is created, making something into an *idol*. This can be the case in Satanism, the worship of the 'beast' or the worship of power, the State or riches: 'You cannot serve God and money' (Mt 6,24).

Ps 115,4f

Rev 13–14

Magic and divination

2115 The future is in the hands of God's providence, and Scripture has consistently condemned those who seek to uncover the course of events by occult means. This would extend to astrology and the consultation of horoscopes, as well as to palmistry and the consultation of mediums in Spiritualism.

Dt 18,10
Jer 29,8
1 Sam 28

2117 It also embraces any use of magic such as lucky charms, and far more so the practice of witchcraft itself, even if this is cloaked in a benevolent guise.

Sacrilege and simony

2118   Those who profane the sacraments, in particular
the Holy Eucharist, or profane places or persons
or objects consecrated to God are guilty of
sacrilege. Those who attempt to buy spiritual gifts   CIC 1367
and benefits which are from God alone follow the   1376
path of Simon the magician who was condemned   Jos 7,11
in the Acts of the Apostles for attempting to do so.   Acts 8,20

2122   The ministers of the Church ask nothing for the
administration of the sacraments, so that the   CIC 848
poorest should not be deprived, but those who   CIC 945
serve at the altar can claim a share from the altar
(1Cor 9,13 – 14); the offering of money to a priest
for Mass is an extension of this principle and
rightly helps to support the clergy.

Atheism and agnosticism

2123   There are many varieties of atheism, which tend to
concentrate either on the material universe to the
exclusion of anything beyond it, or desire to set
man   free,   and   see   religion   as   a   restraint.
Unfortunately, the bad example and inadequate
presentation of the faith have contributed to the
formation of what is seen as one of the gravest
problems of our age. In fact it should be made   GS 19
clear   that   religion   responds   to   the   deepest
yearnings of the human heart, and those who call
themselves agnostics may merit the words of S.   GS 21
Paul 'what therefore you worship as unknown,   Acts 17,23
this I proclaim to you'.

'You shall not make for yourself a graven image'

2129   The prohibition against images of God stems from
the reality of the transcendent God himself, as
revealed at Horeb 'since you saw no form on the
day that the Lord spoke to you' (Dt 4,15).   Num
21,4 – 9

2130   However God did allow the carving of images   Ex
such as the bronze serpent, the ark of the covenant   25,10 – 12
and the cherubim over it. The Church in her turn   Nic II
has allowed images, against the teaching of the   DS 601
iconoclasts, maintaining that he who venerates an

image, venerates the person represented by it and
ultimately God, glorified in his saints.

Aquinas
ST 2–2,81,3

Second Commandment : 'You shall not take the name of the Lord Your God in vain'

2142　At the heart of Revelation is the mysterious
disclosure of God's own name which admits us
into his very presence. His name is holy and it calls
forth that awe which combines love and respect
from every faithful Christian.

Ps 29,2;96,2
113,1–2

Mt 10,32;
1 Tim 6,12

2146　We must not abuse God's name by perjury: 'You
shall not swear falsely, but you shall perform to
the Lord what you have sworn' (Mt 5,33) Instead
we must take our sworn word seriously, as well as
our promises. We must also not misuse the name
of God in blasphemy, whether in swear words or
in calling upon God to justify unworthy and
degrading activity.

Jas 5,12
CIC 1199

CIC 1369

The Christian name

2156　We should remember that when we were baptised,
we received our name in the Name of the Father,
and of the Son and of the Holy Spirit. That name
must not be unworthy of our Christian vocation,
and should be either that of a saint or derived
from a Christian virtue or a mystery of our faith.

CIC 855

2157　We are also signed with the Cross to strengthen us
in our journey through life, so that at length we
can be known as followers of the Lamb in the
kingdom of our Father.

Rev 2,17;
14,1

Third Commandment: 'Remember to keep holy the Sabbath Day'

2168　*The Sabbath* is that day of solemn rest which
commemorates the work of creation: for 'in six
days the Lord made heaven and earth, the sea, and
all that is in them, and rested the seventh day;
therefore the Lord blessed the sabbath day and

Ex 31,15

hallowed it' (Ex 20,11). It is also seen as a memorial of the saving work of God which freed Israel from slavery 'with a mighty hand and an outstretched arm' (Dt 5,15) and made with them a perpetual covenant of which the sabbath would be a continual sign.

Ex 31,16

2172   The Sabbath is given to allow a necessary rest from the labour of the week, so that we can free ourselves from the daily grind of work.

Neh 13,15f
2 Chr 36,21

2173   Jesus was often accused of breaking the sabbath by performing works that were forbidden (cf Mk 3,2; Jn 9,14), but he always observed the sabbath, going 'to the synagogue as his custom was' (Lk 4,16). But he claimed for himself the right to interpret the law as 'Lord of the Sabbath', 'for the Sabbath is made for man, not man for the Sabbath' (Mk 2,27–28).

2174   *Sunday* is for Christians not only the eighth day, or Sabbath, but also the first day because it marks that new creation inaugurated by Christ's resurrection, the Lord's day (cf. dimanche, domingo, doménica).

Mk 16,1
Mt 28,1

2176   Sunday is in truth 'the day that the Lord has made' (Ps 118,24) allowing mankind to give God that public worship which is our recognition of his covenant with us. From earliest times Christians have gathered together on this day to celebrate the Eucharist, 'the foremost holy day of obligation in the universal Church'.

Aquinas
ST 2–2
122,4

CIC 1246

The other days of obligation are Christmas, the Epiphany, the Ascension and the Most Holy Body and Blood of Christ, Holy Mary Mother of God and her Immaculate Conception and Assumption, Saint Joseph, the Apostles Saints Peter and Paul, and All Saints.

2181   The obligation to share in the Eucharist, normally in one's own parish, is a fundamental sign of one's commitment to Christ and his Church and a reinforcement of our faith; and it therefore cannot be omitted without serious rason (e.g. sickness, or the care of very young children).

CIC 515

CIC 1245

2184   As a day of rest, Sunday should allow Christians
to relax in mind and body, so that they can at the
same time engage in the corporal works of mercy   Jas 1,27
(q.v.) and spend time with their families.   CIC 1247

Fourth Commandment: 'Honour your father and your mother'

2197   The Fourth Commandment heads the second list
of commandments relating to the love of neighbour, starting with the family and radiating out to
human life, marriage, material goods ...

The family in God's plan

2201   Marriage and family life are structures for the
good of the spouses and the procreation and
education of their children. They are seen in the
light of Christian revelation, as reflecting the
communion between Father, Son and Holy Spirit   Eph 5,21f
and a copy of that greater mystery between Jesus   LG 11
and his holy people, so that the family can be   FC 21
called a 'domestic Church'.   GS 52

The family and society

2207   Family life is that natural community in which
authority, stability and mutual love give rise to the
bases of freedom, security and friendship, which
are at the heart of society itself. The larger social
group depends for its well-being on the family,
and must uphold its rights intact. These include   GS 47.52
the right to raise a family and educate them
according to one's religious convictions; the right
to profess one's faith and educate one's children
in it; the right to private property; the right to
work; the right to emigrate; the right to health
care; protection against the dangers of drugs,
alcoholism and pornography; the right to form   FC 46
family groups and to have civic representation;
the right to have the stability of marriage and the
institution of the family itself upheld.

Duties of members of the family

2214   *The duty of children* towards their parents stems   Sir 7,27f
from gratitude. It calls for obedience in the young,   Col 3,20
who are enabled to advance in wisdom and age and
grace (this extends also to those who take the place
of parents). In those who have reached their   Sir 3,2f
majority there is an obligation to care for parents,
especially in their old age, an attentiveness so
praised by Jesus himself (Mk 7,10–12). Christians
especially should respect those who have handed
on the faith to them and encouraged it to grow.   2 Tim 1,5

2221   *The duty of parents* extends to the whole field of
education both moral and spiritual. As the first
heralds of the faith, they are the ministers of that   LG 11
faith to their children, so that they can grow in
virtue and holiness (hence the importance of the
truly Christian school) and come to choose their   VS 116
profession and raise a family, or accept a religious
vocation, with its charism of celibacy.   Mt 10,37

The duties of civil authorities and of their citizens

2235   According to Christ's teaching, authority must be
seen as service, which the superiors exercise with   Mt 20,26
wisdom, respecting the rights of each, and the
civil freedom all individuals possess in the
interests of the common good. The citizens in their   CA 25
turn should respect their superiors, for they 'have
been instituted by God' (Rom 13,1). Love of one's
country, which includes the obligation of coming
to the country's defence, stems from both
gratitude and charity. The duty of paying taxes
and exercising the right to vote comes from one's
civil responsibility.   Rom 13,7

2243   This does not rule out just criticism of authority,
and even the refusal of obedience when there are   Acts 5,29
long and grave violations of human rights, when all
other means have been exhausted, when there is a
well-founded hope of success and it will not provoke
worse results, and there is no better solution.

The Church and the political community

2244   Most societies respect the value of the individual,
but only divine revelation safeguards the trans-

cendence of the human person, because it sees man coming from God and going to him. The Church therefore reserves to itself the right to intervene when fundamental human rights or the salvation of souls are at stake, using only those means which are however in accordance with the precepts of the Gospel. CA 45,46

GS 76

Fifth Commandment: 'You shall not kill'

Respect for human life: human life is sacred

2258 Revelation tells us of the sacredness of human life from the dawn of history, by reminding us that blood is a sacred sign of life and to shed it, as Cain shed the blood of Abel, cries to heaven. Sacred Scripture emphasises that it is forbidden to slay the innocent and righteous (Ex 23,7), and Jesus extends this to include any act of anger or vengeance. Lev 17,14 Gen 4,8–12 Gen 9,5–6 CDF Donum Vitae 5 Mt 5,21f Mt 26,52

2263 In self-defence, one can resist an aggressor even to the extent of causing his death, 'the action of defending oneself *could have a double effect*: one being the preservation of one's own life, the other being the death of the aggressor; only one is wished.' The same principle applies to the State's right to impose penalties on those found guilty of crimes (so that they can atone for their faults and also make amends); and, if such sanctions are not sufficient, ultimately to impose the death penalty. Aquinas ST 2–2 64, Lk 23,40f

Voluntary murder

2268 The fifth commandment condemns any direct and voluntary murder as a crime which calls to heaven for vengeance. Those who cooperate are equally guilty, even if they cite eugenic or health reasons. Similarly, it is forbidden to put the life of anyone at risk without grave reason, or to create conditions which lead to death through starvation and poverty. Am 8,4f

Abortion

2270 Life is sacred from the moment of conception, and the human being possesses the inalienable

right to exist. Those who deprive an innocent
unborn human being of life by direct abortion are
guilty of an abominable crime and incur auto-   GS 51
matic excommunication.   CIC 1398

2274   Surgical interventions at the embryonic stage,
with the purpose of bettering the chance of
survival or future health are quite licit, but it is
forbidden to exploit human embryos in the cause   CDF
of science and to engage in any genetic manipu-   Donum
lation, for these go against the dignity and rights   Vitae 1
of the individual.

Euthanasia

2276   The elderly, the disturbed and the sick are entitled   GS 27
to live out their lives with dignity. Any attempt to   VS 80
cause their death, by euthanasia, either directly or
by omission is gravely wrong. Thus ordinary
treatments should not be withdrawn, because
these provide that legitimate comfort to which
human beings are entitled in their last hours. This
does not mean that extraordinary means need be
taken, or that medicines which eventually bring
about death should be denied if their aim is the
alleviation of pain.

Suicide

2280   We are not Lords of our own life, but
administrators of the life which God has given us.   CDF JB
Suicide goes against the natural inclination of that
love we owe to ourselves, as well as injuring the
relationship which we should have with our   Rom 14,8
family, our neighbours and the society in which
we live. Those who assist anyone to commit
suicide are equally guilty.

2282   Although suicide is especially painful when it
occurs among young people, and creates a
scandal, there is often diminished responsibility
due to psychological disturbance, suffering, or
intense pain. We must not despair of those who
commit suicide, because final repentance is always
possible, nor should we judge, but rather
commend them to Our Lady of Sorrows.

Respect for the dignity of individuals

2284   *Scandal* is an attack against the soul of one's
neighbour which is every bit as damaging as any
material wound. Christ compared the pharisees in
their scandalous conduct to wolves, and said that
those who caused little ones, who believed in him,   Mt 7,15
to sin, deserved to be drowned in the depths of the   Lk 17,1
sea (Mt 18,6).   1 Cor 8,

2288   *Health*, like life, is a gift of God and must be
cherished. This of necessity involves the virtue of
temperance (q.v.) so that any worship of the body
is avoided. On a different level, we must not abuse
our health by addiction to overeating, over-
drinking, smoking; and drugs which have no
therapeutic use.

2293   Scientific experiments on individuals are often
needed to assess the viability of new research, but
these must be in accord with the dignity of man
himself, even if the individual consents. The
mutilation or possible death of one person is not
justified by the gift of health to a recipient of an
organ transplant.

2297   *Physical integrity*, which should be respected,
forbids mutilation and direct sterilisation, as well
as torture, hijacking, kidnapping and the taking
of hostages.   DS 3722

2299   *Respect for the dead* is shown by the Church in its
funeral rites which honour those who are temples
of the Holy Spirit committed to the arms of the
Good Shepherd.

2301   Cremation is allowed by the Church, unless it has
been chosen to indicate a denial of the resurrection
of the body.   CIC 117

The protection of peace

2302   Christ who is our peace (Eph 2,14) demands of us
that we eliminate all hatred and anger from our
hearts, so that we can love our enemies and have   Mt 5,2
that mutual respect which is the work of justice

and the fruit of charity. The alternative has so often been the scourge of war, which can now inflict devastation on a scale undreamt of, largely upon the innocent.   GS 78

2307 However, war can be justified if all peaceful means have been exhausted, but the principles to be observed have already been stated under the citizen's right to refuse obedience to authority. Here they are called: the principles of *a just war*. Those who serve in the armed forces work for the common good of the nation and the maintenance of peace. In time of war those who object to military service should do some other community service, while those who take up arms are not free to use any means they choose in combat, nor is an indiscriminate and excessive bombardment   GS 80 justified by the fact of hostilities.

2315 The arms race is one of the greatest curses of our day, it does not eliminate war, but rather makes it more likely. Nations must work to eradicate it, so that swords can indeed be beaten into   GS 81 ploughshares.   Is 2,4

Sixth Commandment: 'You shall not commit adultery'

2331 In the beginning God 'created man in his own image, ... male and female he created them. And God blessed them, and God said to them, "Be fruitful and multiply"' (Gen 1,27–28). He thus makes them sharers in his own communion of love, giving them the capacity for love which is   Gen 5,1–2 able to bring forth new life.   FC 11

2332 In creating the human race male and female, God gives to man and woman an equal dignity which requires of those with a vocation to the married   FC 22 state, that they live out their sexual identity in harmony, helping them to complement each other, and by becoming one flesh to achieve the will of the Creator.   Gen 2,24

2336 This original design was restored by Christ, who   Mt 5,27–28 extended the sixth commandment to include the   Mt 19,6 heart's desires and thus the whole of human sexuality.

The vocation to chastity

2337 Chastity deals with the integration of the powers of life and love which we all possess, giving us that true unity which belongs to our dignity as persons made to share in the love of God.

Aug
Conf 10,29

2341 Chastity forms part of the cardinal virtue of *temperance* by which we learn to dominate our passions by the practice of the moral virtues, obedience to the commandments, prayer and reception of the sacraments, so that our passions do not dominate us. It is a work that lasts all one's life, and requires that constant choice of the good, in resistance to the temptation to give way to weakness. In that struggle for self-control we can rely on the gift of the Holy Spirit who works from the moment of our baptism to bring us that love of God which allows us to give of ourselves in imitation of Him who gave himself even to the end, out of love for us.

Sir 1,22
GS 17
Tit 2,1–6

Gal 5,22

Jn 13,1;
15,5

2348 As we have put on Christ, so we are called to crucify the flesh with its passions and desires. This is the case whether we are called to the state of consecrated celibacy or virginity, whether we are single or married, or indeed engaged to be married.

Gal 3,27;
5,24

Ambrose
vid 23

Offences against Chastity

2351 In our present fallen condition people erroneously equate sex with love. The Church has always taught that seeking sensual pleasure for itself is a grave distortion of love, and sinful. In this sense *masturbation*, the voluntary arousal of the genital organs for pleasure has always been considered intrinsically wrong. The culpability may easily be diminished because it has become a habit or it has arisen out of anxiety and stress. *Fornication* which takes place outside marriage is gravely sinful because it goes against an essential purpose of human sexuality which is the generation and

CDF
PH 9

education of children by their own parents. *Pornography*, which deals with the exhibition of sexual activity, belittles the sexual act and degrades those who take part in it, or use it. As it can lead people into sin, authorities should act against it. *Prostitution* is a grave sin and a social scandal for those who give themselves to it because in so doing they dishonour their own bodies. But the practice of prostitution is often resorted to because of poverty or blackmail which reduce its culpability. *Rape* is not only a sexual   1 Cor 6,15f violation but also an assault on someone's personal integrity. It is graver still when it is a question of child abuse or incest because, these sins are committed by people in positions of trust. *Homosexual* activity has always been considered   Gen in Scripture as a serious depravity, and in the   19,1–29 Tradition of the Church as contrary to natural   Rom law, because it lacks both that essential sexual   1,24–27; complementariness of man and woman or the   1 Cor 6,10; procreative potential. The cause of homosexuality   1 Tim 1,10 may be partly genetic and partly psychological;   CDF there is a danger that people may be thrust into   PH 8 homosexual activity by a permissive culture and it needs to be stated that an orientation, however culturally perceived is not sinful and indeed, lived out chastely it is a path to holiness.

The love of spouses

2360   The sexual union of a man and a woman in marriage is 'by no means something purely biological, but concerns the innermost being of the human person as such. It is realized in a truly human way only if it is an integral part of the love by which a man and a woman commit themselves totally to one another until death.' Their love expressed in this way signifies and expresses that mutual gift of themselves which is life-giving and   FC 11 permanent.   GS 49

2364   The covenant that married people freely enter into   CIC 1056 imposes a permanent obligation of fidelity taken up into that mystery of Christ who is faithful to his Church, and who declares that what God has joined, no man can put asunder.   Mk 10,9

2366   Married love naturally tends to be *creative of life*. Children come from the mutual gift of oneself in love. This is the reason that the Church cannot break the connection between the unitive and procreative meaning of the marriage act. The spouses are called to cooperate in the love of God the Creator who through them enriches his family.

HV 12
Pius XI
Casti Con.
DS 3717
GS 50

2368   If married couples wish to regulate the number of their children, they can make use of methods which depend upon observation of the menstrual cycle and the periods of natural infertility. These methods allow an openness to procreation, respect the integrity of each other's sexuality, and encourage a growth in chastity. The State has no power to force birth control policies on their population, because the regulation of the size of families is the personal concern of the parents themselves.

HV 14

HV 16
PP 37
HV 23

2372   Children are a great blessing for parents, but they are a gift and not a right. Those who are unfortunately incapable of having children deserve all our compassion, but sterility must not be seen as something evil, rather as a share in Christ's Cross; it is also an invitation to make a home for an abandoned child, or take up some work for God and his Church.

Gen 30,1

2376   Medical techniques which allow married couples to have children without sexual relations are not regarded as licit by the Church. In the case of artificial insemination by donor (AID) and *in-vitro* fertilisation and the use of surrogate mothers, these are gravely sinful, depriving as they do the child of the right to be born of married love. The Church also reproves those who have recourse to artificial insemination of the wife by the sperm of the husband because procreation must be the result of the marriage act itself, the fruit of their love.

CDF
Donum
Vitae 2
CDF
Donum
Vitae 82

Offences against the dignity of marriage

Hos 2,7

2380   The prophets denounced *adultery* as akin to idolatry, and Christ forbade even the lustful desire

Jer 5,7;
13,27

as adultery of the heart. The reason for the
condemnation is that adultery is a crime against
the rights of each partner to have that undivided
love that they promised before God.

Mt 5,27–28

2382 *Divorce* which was conceded by Moses because of
man's hardness of heart in not accepting the
original precept of God, was condemned by Jesus,
who reiterated the indissolubility of marriage. The
Church continues to maintain that a sacramentally valid and consummated union cannot be
dissolved. Those who remarry commit adultery,
causing harm to the partner they have left, to any
children there may be and to society, of which the
family is a vital and living cell.

Mt 19,7–9

CIC 1141

Mt 19,9

2386 *Separation* can be a painful solution to a marriage
which becomes unworkable and this can involve a
civil divorce without any culpability attached.
There is similarly no culpability attached to the
innocent party of a divorce, who should be
supported by the local parishioners in remaining
faithful, especially when this involves bringing up
a family alone.

CIC 1151f

2387 *Polygamy* is against the moral law 'because it is
contrary to the equal personal dignity of men and
women who in matrimony give themselves with a
love that is total and therefore unique and
exclusive'. Those who have been polygamous
incur an obligation towards their former wives
and children when they become monogamous.

FC 19

2388 *Incest* and *child abuse* have already been treated
under *rape*. It is forbidden under the old law and,
specifically repudiated by S. Paul.

Lev 18,7f
1 Cor 5,1.4

2390 *Co-habiting, trial marriages* and other variations
are grave sins amounting to an offence against the
very fidelity of marriage, which demands a total
and definitive gift of oneself. Those who are in
such a state cannot receive Holy Communion until
they regularise their situation.

PH 7
FC 80

Seventh Commandment: 'You shall not steal'

2401 We are bound by the seventh commandment to respect the goods of others, but at the same time as we put a value on private property we need to remember that the riches of the earth are given to all. We must play our part in working for a just distribution of wealth.   Ex 20,15 Dt 5,19 Mt 19,18

Private property

2402 Private property is a right that guarantees a measure of security and dignity to people so that they can be freed from poverty and can raise a family of their own. But the fruits of creation are meant to be shared by all, and the State has the right to regulate this for the common good. The individual should therefore regard what he possesses not as exclusively his own, but as given to him to benefit others apart from himself.   GS 71 CA 40.48 GS 69

2403 We have a duty both to manage agricultural, industrial or technological production so that everyone benefits, and to use things moderately so that we can share it with those in greatest need, for Christ 'being rich made himself poor that he might enrich us with his poverty' (2 Cor 8,9).

Respect for the goods of others

2408 *Robbery* is any illegal taking of the goods of others against the reasonable wishes of the owner. This would extend to commercial fraud, retention of goods that have been borrowed or have been mislaid, paying unjust salaries and tampering with prices as well as passing false cheques or credit cards, over-inflating property values, embezzlement, and obtaining money by false pretences.   Dt 25, 13,16 Dt 24,14f Jas 5,4 Am 8,4-6 VS 100

2410 *Promises and Contracts* need to be scrupulously observed and entered into in good faith. They are regulated by *commutative justice*.

2411 *Legal* justice regulates what the citizen owes to the community; *distributive* justice regulates what the community owes to each citizen.

It is by virtue of commutative justice that we are bound to make *reparation* for any injustice committed, by restoring the property or its value to the owner, after the example of Zacchaeus.   Lk 19,8

2414 It is against all morality to treat people as merchandise to be bought and sold, stealing their dignity from them and reducing them to the level of slaves.

2413 Gambling, if it is a question of large sums, which have an impact on an individual's ability to live a normal life and support himself and his family, is sinful, and both an addiction and an enslavement.

2415 *Respect for the whole of creation* is a duty imposed upon us as having 'dominion over all the earth' (Gen 1,26.28). That dominion implies that   CL 43
we must respect the delicate balance of the   GS 36
environment for its own sake and that of future   CA 37–38
generations. The animals in particular are objects   Mt 6,16
of God's providence and give him glory, and we   Dan 3,
have no right to make them suffer wantonly.   57–58

2417 It is quite lawful to use animals for food or clothing or to tame them to perform certain tasks, or to use them in medical experiments which will benefit humanity, or to have them as pets, but they must not be idolised as if they were human.

The Church's social teaching

2421 This evolved in the nineteenth century with the rise of the modern industrial society. The principal documents are *Rerum Novarum* (1891), *Quadragesimo Anno* (1931), *Mater et Magistra* (1961), *Pacem in Terris* (1963), *Gaudium et Spes* (1965), *Populorum Progressio* (1967) *Octogesima Adveniens* (1971), *Laborem Exercens* (1981), *Sollicitudo Rei Socialis* (1988) and *Centesimus Annus* (1991).

They teach that you cannot run society merely by economic criteria, reducing the work-force to   CA 24
items on the profit and loss account.   GS 65

2425 The Church rejects all collective systems which reduce people to means of production, whether communist or socialist, capitalist or individualist. The concept of regulating the economy by market forces is also opposed, because such a theory takes no account of the common good and the need in consequence to regulate the market. CA 10.34.44

Social justice and economic activity

2426 God commanded our first parents to 'fill the earth and subdue it' (Gen 1,28) and this is brought about by *human labour*, which is both a duty for mankind and a tribute to God the creator, who remains the master of the work of his hands, and not its slave. It is also redemptive in union with Jesus the carpenter, who allows us to unite our human toil with his divine work. 2 Thes 3,10 GS 34; CA 31 LE 27

2430 *Economic life* is often a field of opposing interests, and because of this it is vital to maintain the right of both individual and group initiative, as well as the means for negotiation between competing interests. At the same time, the intervention of the State assures some guarantee of individual freedom, stable currency and efficient public services 'so that those who work and produce can enjoy the fruits of their labours and thus feel encouraged to work efficiently and honestly'. *Management* bear the responsibility for the well-being of their employees and the impact of their productivity on the environment, as well as for the interests of their shareholders, who allow access to working capital for future development. *Workers* have the right to employment regardless of race, sex and handicap and also to receive a just salary. They also enjoy the right to *strike*, provided this is not accompanied by violence and is linked directly to conditions in the work-place; management is not entitled to operate a lock-out policy in retaliation, which is an assault on the dignity of the person. LE 11 CA 48 LE 19f Lev 19,13 Dt 24,14f LE 18

Justice and solidarity between nations

2437 The gap between those who accumulate wealth and those who accumulate debt grows ever

greater. This can only be solved on an international scale by changing the financial system, SRS 14
which holds the poorer nations to ransom, by
means of unjust commercial cartels and the arms SRS 17
trade, as well as the international debt provisions. CA 35

2439 *Rich nations* have a duty in charity and solidarity
to help those who do not themselves have the
means to develop their own economy. It is often
an obligation also in justice, because the rich
nations have profited in the past at the expense of
their poorer neighbours. *International aid* can be
a targeted response in time of local disaster, but in
the long term the international institutions need to
be reformed so that they encourage the under-
developed countries and assist them to become SRS 16
self-sufficient. Ultimately the end of exploitation
and poverty will only come about by a gradual
transformation of the whole of society, absorbing CA 26
the message which Christ preached and died for. CA 51

2442 The pastors of the Church are not called upon to
make political statements and take part in political
activity, because this is properly the arena of lay
people acting as the leaven in society. Clerics
should not be actively involved in political parties SRS 47
or trade unions for the same reason. CIC 287

Love for the poor

2443 Jesus came to proclaim Good News to the poor,
lived in poverty himself, sent out his followers in Mt 11,5
poverty, and recognised 'the blessed of his Father' Mt 8,20
as those who had ministered to him in the poor. Mt 10,8
The Church has constantly professed the need to Mt
love the poor and to share one's riches with them. 25,31–36
'If we do not share our riches with the poor, we CA 57
are robbing them and draining their life from Jas 5,1–6
them. What we possess is not our own possession Chrys
but it belongs to them'. Laz 1,6

2447 *The works of mercy* may be *spiritual* (instructing,
counselling, comforting, forgiving, suffering
wrongs and praying) or *corporal*, which consist in
feeding the hungry, giving drink to the thirsty,
clothing the naked, giving a roof to the homeless,

visiting the sick and imprisoned and burying the dead. Many of these works centre around the poor, and we are urged by Jesus himself to 'give alms from what you have and, look, everything will be clean for you' (Lk 11,41). This only took up the earlier prescriptions of the Old Testament: 'For the poor will never cease out of the land; therefore I command you, you shall open wide your hand to your brother, to the needy and to the poor in the land' (Dt 15,11; cf Jn 12,8). In response to this, the Church continues its work of service to the poor, seeing in them Christ himself.

2449 The Old Testament provided a series of laws to help the poor: the Jubilee to forgive debt; the prohibition of interest on loans, the withholding of pledges, the obligation of the tithe, daily pay for labourers and the right to glean after the harvest.

Eighth Commandment: 'You shall not bear false witness'

2465 The Old Testament proclaims that God's word stands firm for ever, his truth lasts from age to age (Ps 119,90) and for this reason Israel is called to choose the way of truth. That truth was made flesh in Jesus, the Word of God, the light come into the world that mankind might not walk in darkness, but in the light of his truth, which brings true freedom. It is through the Spirit of Truth that the Father sends, in Jesus' name, that we can be consecrated and led to know the fulness of truth.

Prov 8,7
2 Sam 7,28
Rom 3,4
Jn 8,12; 12,46
Jn 8,31
Jn 17,17
16,13

2468 Truthfulness or veracity is a natural yearning in mankind which in fact makes ordinary human relationships possible, based as they are on that balance between telling the truth and keeping things confidential. In addition, the Christian is urged to 'speak the truth with (one's) neighbour, for we are members one of another' (Eph 4,25) and never ought to be ashamed of bearing witness to the truth.

DH 2
Aquinas
ST 2-2
109, 3
Mt 5,37
2 Tim 1,8

2471   Although all Christians are called *to bear witness* to the truth of the Gospel, 'having a clear conscience before God and men' (Acts 24,16), the   AG 11
Church has always regarded the *martyr* as the   VS 89
supreme witness for the truth of the faith in every age, because he bears witness to the truth in his own blood.

Offences against the truth

2476   *False witness and perjury*, when they are committed publicly have a particular gravity   Prov 19,9
which earned condemnation in the Old Testament. It undermines the exercise of justice, allowing the innocent to be found guilty and the guilty to go free in extreme cases, and obstructs the course of justice in others.   Prov 18,5

2477   *Rash judgement* is that sinful acceptance of the   CIC 220
truth about someone's moral defects without any   Sir 21,28
foundation for them. *Slander* is the revelation of   Is 33,15
such defects to others and *calumny* the falsification of the reputation of another. Everyone has a right to their reputation in justice and charity and we are told repeatedly by the Saints that we must make allowances for others rather than apportion blame.

2480   At the same time we must avoid *flattery*, especially when it effectively makes one an accomplice in another's sin. Friendship should not stoop to hypocrisy. It is also false in us to boast and indulge in excessive irony; both are in fact *lies*.

2482   The gravity of *lying* is measured against the truth which it distorts, the circumstances which surround it, the intentions at the time and the   Aug
consequences. Any deliberate intention to deceive   Mend 4,5
is gravely sinful and ultimately comes from the devil, the father of lies (Jn 8,44). It is a crime against the truth and undermines the whole structure of society, by calling trust into question. There is a strict obligation to make reparation for the damage caused.

Confidentiality

2488   The right to information is not unconditional. There is a competing right to confidentiality: 'Whoever betrays secrets destroys confidence' (Sir 27, 16). The individual in his private or public life is entitled to privacy and the media have to weigh carefully the public's right to know and the person's entitlement to discretion.

Prov 25, 9–10

Sir 42,1

2490   *The secret of the 'seal of Confession'* can never be revealed, whatever the circumstances, under pain of excommunication reserved to the Holy See. Other *professional secrets* should be respected and should only be revealed to avoid far worse consequences.

CIC 983

The communications media

2494   Society has a right to information founded on truth, charity, and justice, and the communications media play an important and ever increasing role in this regard.

IM 5; 11

2496   The individual consumer of the mass media (viewer, listener) must exercise discipline and circumspection to avoid becoming a passive receiver of stimuli. Those who report for the media have a responsibility to serve the truth and not to pass the limits of charity leading to defamation. The State has the duty of supporting the freedom of the media instead of manipulating it for its own ends, or allowing it to be so used. But it should also penalise any unwarranted invasion of privacy.

IM 12

Truth, beauty and sacred art

2500   Truth is beautiful in itself because it brings to the mind the knowlege of things created and uncreated. God also reveals himself through the beauty of his creation, since he is the very source of its splendour. Mankind, through art expresses a talent which comes from God the Creator and reflects his work in the measure that it leads us to glorify him through the artist's creation. This is

Wis 13,3

eminently true of sacred art, that aspires to be at
the same time splendid, and totally in accord with   SC
the faith and the liturgy.   122–127

Ninth Commandment : 'You shall not covet your neighbour's wife'

2514   S. John talks of three types of lust: the flesh, the
eyes and the pride of life (I Jn 2,16). The ninth   Gal 5,16f
commandment forbids lust of the flesh and the   Eph 2,3
tenth greed for the goods of others.   DS 1515

Purity of heart

2517   The struggle against the lust of the flesh begins in
the heart, for 'from the heart come evil thoughts,
murder, adultery, fornication, theft, false
witness, slander' (Mt 15,19). This is why the sixth
beatitude proclaims 'Blessed are the pure in heart'
(Mt 5,8) for they are given that singleness of
purpose which links love, chastity and orthodox
faith: 'believing we obey God; obeying we live
worthily; living worthily, we purify our heart and   Aug
purifying our heart, we understand what we   fid et symb
believe'. Such purity of heart enables us even now   10,25
to anticipate that final vision of God face to face. 1 Cor 13,12

The struggle for purity

2520   The whole of our life is a struggle against the lust
of the flesh, which God joins through the gifts of
his grace and the virtue of chastity. This struggle
needs purity of intention, which seeks what is truly
the will of God in all things, custody of the eyes;
and prayer.   Wis 15,5

2521   Purity also demands *modesty*, which preserves a
certain delicacy relating to sexual matters. It
cultivates a respect for the spiritual dignity of man
and woman which should be removed from
exhibitionism and eroticism giving them the   cf. Jer 6,15
freedom to love God in each other.   GS 58

2526   Sex education should allow young people to know
the value of human sexuality and the need

for maturity and self-control, so that they can learn how the use of sex in marriage must be the expression of a generous and creative love in a life- PV 44
long union, life-giving through self giving.

Tenth Commandment : 'You shall not covet your neighbour's goods

The disorder of concupiscence

2535 The Tenth Commandment forbids *avarice* and the desire born of that lust for riches and the power which they give, 'No one who loves money ever RC 3,10,13
has enough' (Eccl 5, 9). It is a desire that has to be constantly watched, because it masquerades frequently as commercial initiative. Similarly the tenth commandment forbids *envy* which is a form of sadness of heart. We are told that death entered the world through the devil's envy, and it was the root of both David's fall and that of Ahab. It was Wis 2,24
also 'out of envy' that Jesus was delivered up. 2 Sam
Such a sin must be met by charity, to overcome the 12,1–4
sadness; the charity which belongs to the sons of 1 K 21, 1f
God who are led by his Spirit to put to death the Mt 27,18
deeds of the body and crucify the flesh with its Rom 8,14
passions and desires. Gal 5,24

Poverty of heart

2544 Jesus puts before his disciples that total gift of oneself which involves renouncing all that we have, and giving all that we have. The poor widow Lk 14,33;
measured up to the challenge, while the rich young 18,2
man did not. At the root lies a trust in God's Lk 21,4
providence and his kingdom rather than in the Lk 18,22
consolation provided by possessions. 'Where our Mt 6,25 – 34
treasure is, there is our heart also' (Lk 12, 34) and Lk 6,24
with the help of God the Christian must see that the possession of God, and communion with him, is true wealth, and worth all the struggle for holiness "There shall be the true glory of the future; nobody will be praised there for error or for flattery; true honours will neither be denied to those who deserve them or granted to those who are unworthy of them, for there only those who

are worthy will be admitted to enter. There true peace will hold sway in which nobody will be disturbed either interiorly or from anyone else. The reward of virtue will be God himself who is the source of virtue and who has promised to give himself as the greatest reward that could be conceived: 'I will be your God and you will be my people' (Lev 26,12) ... This is also the meaning of the apostle when he says 'so that God may be all in all' (1 Cor 15, 28). He will be the end of our desires, who shall be gazed upon without end, loved without surfeit and praised without weariness. And this gift, this love, this enjoyment will be, surely, as the eternal life, common to all." Aug civ Dei 22,30

Part Four:
Christian Prayer

2558 The Church professes her faith in the Symbol of the Apostles (Part One) and celebrates that faith in the Liturgy (Part Two), so that it might be lived out in the Church (Part Three) within a personal and living relationship with God, Father, Son and Holy Spirit (Part Four).

What is prayer?

2559 Prayer, which is the raising up of the mind to God, is above all that great gift of God, whose worth we need to discover, in humility of heart. We thirst for God and God thirsts to give us living water, welling up to eternal life. In the depths of our being (which Scripture calls *the heart* more than a thousand times) we allow that conversation to take place, prompted by the Holy Spirit in union with Christ and in his body the Church, directed to the Father in one communion of love.

John Dam
FO 3,24
Jn 4,10
Rom 8,26
Ps 130,14
Acts 17,27
VS 65

Section I: The Revelation of Prayer and the Universal Vocation to Pray

Chapter 1   In the Old Testament

2568   The Revelation of Prayer in the Old Testament takes place between the fall of man and his restoration to grace. It is enclosed between God saying 'Where are you ... What have you done?' (Gen 3,9,13) and the Son of Man saying when he came into the world 'Behold I have come to do your will' (Heb 10,5,7).

2569   In the early chapters of Genesis we see prayer expressed as part of the fabric of the creation itself as related to the Creator. Abel gives voice to this by offering the first-born of his flock (Gen 4, 4); Noah's offering is found pleasing to God who blesses creation again in him, and establishes an everlasting covenant, reminding mankind of the Creator so that they may call upon him and finally walk with him. 'Abraham believed God' (Jas 2, 23) summarises the attitude of the patriarch, our father in faith. He went out from his country and his father's house, 'as the Lord had told him' (Gen 12, 4) without words, but walking before God, to whom he built an altar at every step of his journey. Abraham had that trust in the word of God which persisted when childless, and endured even to the extent of not hesitating to offer to God his son in obedience, 'considering that God was powerful enough even to raise the dead to life', like the Almighty Father who did not spare his own Son. He also had that same compassion which Jesus was to show when he interceded for sinners knowing that God heard him and blessed him. This persevering prayer was exemplified in *Jacob*, the father of the twelve tribes, who wrestled all night until the breaking of the day until he received God's blessing.

Gen 8,20f
Gen 9,15
Gen 426
Gen 5,24
MR
EP I. 95
Gen 17,1
Gen 12,7
8;13,18
Gen 15,6
Heb 11,17
Heb 11,19
Rom 8,32
Heb 5,7
Gen 18,16f
Heb 7,1f
cf Jn 11, 42

Gen 32,24f

2574   *Moses* is called from the midst of the burning bush
to be the means of the divine compassion and to
accomplish the salvation of Israel: 'He sanctified
him through faithfulness and meekness; he chose
him out of all mankind. He made him hear his
voice' (Sir 45:4–5). He was chosen to speak with
God 'as a man with his friend' (Ex 33, 11) and to
transmit the word of God to the people,   Ps 106,23
interceding for them again and again, relying on
the promises that God had made 'a God merciful
and gracious, slow to anger, and abounding in
steadfast love and faithfulness' (Ex 34, 6).

2578   The people themselves are taught to pray 'in the
presence of God' who dwells among them, so
Hannah prayed at Shiloh, so *Samuel* was taught to
pray by Eli, 'Speak, Lord, for your servant is
listening' (1 Sam 3, 9). *David*, the shepherd of his
people, who was chosen to be King of Israel, gives
in the psalms a model of praise and sorrow and   Sir 47,8
blessing which was to be revealed in its fulness in
Christ the Son of David.

2580   *Solomon*, in dedicating the Temple, recalls the
promises of God and asks for forgiveness as well
as divine protection, so that all the nations might
know that Israel was the Lord's inheritance. The
Temple with its liturgy, its sacrifices, its incense
and its feasts would be a constant reminder of the
Glory of God and a call to prayer, joined to the
preaching of the prophets who urged that
conversion of heart without which prayer can lose
its savour.

2581   *Elijah*, who arose 'like a fire' (Sir 48, 1), is granted
the reward of his prayer when he raises the widow   1 K 17,7–24
of Sareptha's son to life and the victory over the   1 K
prophets of Baal on Mount Carmel. His words   18,20–39
'Answer me, O Lord, answer me!' are part of the
epiclesis in the Eastern Eucharistic liturgies. He is
also given the privilege of seeing the presence of
God in the sound of silence from his hiding place   1 K 19,1–14
in the cave at Horeb. The fulness of that glory will   Ex 33,19–23
be glimpsed again on the mount of Trans-
figuration when it shines in Christ who comes   Lk 9,30–35
accompanied by Moses and Elijah.   2 Cor 4,6

2584   The prayer of the prophets is drawn from their meeting with God face to face. They do not retreat from the world in their prayer, but in fact wrestle with God and look forward in eager anticipation for the coming of the Lord of history.

Am 7,2.5;
Is 6,5.8.1.
Jer 1,6;
15,15−18;
20,7−18

2585   *The Psalms* were gathered together into five books representing the essence of Israel's prayer (there are other prayers: Esd 9, 6−15; Neh 1, 4−11; Jon 2, 3−10; Tob 3,11−16; Jud 9, 2−14). They were used at all the great feasts in Jerusalem and later, on the sabbath in the synagogue. They deal with the saving events of Israel's history, the promises of God and the hope of the coming Messiah, but speak in terms that reach into the heart of everyone, because they reveal the whole human drama from creation to its last end, which is a hymn of praise to God, and fittingly ends with *Alleluia* (Praise the Lord!). Christ even from the Cross prays 'My God, my God, why have you forsaken me?' which ends with the words 'You are my praise in the great assembly ... All the earth shall remember and return to the Lord, all families of the nations worship before him for the kingdom is the Lord's; he is ruler of the nations. They shall worship him, all the mighty of the earth; before him shall bow all who go down to the dust.' (Psalm 22, 1.26−30). The Church in the *Liturgy of the Hours* uses the psalms as the heart of the prayer which in Christ she offers to the Father.

Mt 27,46

In the fulness of time

Because Jesus 'reflects the glory of God and bears the very stamp of his nature' (Heb 1, 3), his prayer allows us a glimpse of the holiness of the Trinity. We should first consider how the evangelists tell us about the prayer of Jesus, then listen to his own teaching and how our own prayer is received.

Chapter 2: Jesus prays

2599   Jesus, 'born of woman, born under the law' (Gal 4, 4), learnt from his Virgin Mother how to turn to

God in prayer before he came to know the worship of his people in the synagogue at Nazareth and in the Temple. His prayer was revealed to his mother when he was twelve years old, as having a deeper source: 'Did you not know that I must be engaged in my Father's business' (Lk 2, 49) (other authorities say 'my Father's house'). Jesus prays to the Father as only-begotten *Son*, conscious of the mission given to him by his Father, which was his very food. He therefore prays even before the Father bears witness to him in his baptism in the Jordan, before choosing the apostles, and before Peter proclaims him 'The Christ of God'. He also prays before his Transfiguration, prays that Peter's faith will not fail and in his agony that prayer was bathed with a sweat of blood. He often spent whole nights in prayer (Mc 1, 35. 6, 46; Lk 5,16).

Jn 4,34
Lk 3,21
Lk 6,12
Lk 9,20
Lk 9,28
Lk 22,32
Lk 22,41f

2603   Two occasions on which Jesus prayed have been recorded in greater details by the evangelists. In the first (Mt 11, 25–27; Lk 10, 21–23) which is connected with the mission of the seventy disciples, Jesus begins by blessing and thanking the Father 'for hiding these things from the wise and the prudent and revealing them to babes' (Lk 10, 21). There is an added emphasis in his 'Yes, Father' which reveals that loving union of will. The second prayer takes place before the raising of Lazarus, when Jesus lifts up his eyes and says 'Father, I thank you that you have heard me. I know that you hear me always, but I have said this on account of the people standing by, that they may believe that you sent me' (Jn 11, 41–42). The prayer of Jesus is something constant, a living conversation which is filled with grateful acceptance of the goodness of the Father.

2605   We rightly have a devotion to the *seven last words* which Jesus uttered on Calvary. They are his last testament to humanity: 'Father, forgive them, for they know not what they do' (Lk 23, 34); 'I promise you, today you shall be with me in paradise' (Lk 24, 43); 'Mother, behold your son – Son, behold your Mother' (Jn 19,26–27, 'I thirst' (Jn 19,28) 'My God, my God, why have you forsaken me?' (Mk 15, 34; Ps 22,2); 'It is finished' (Jn 19,30); 'Father, into your hands, I commend my spirit' (Mk 15, 37; Jn 19, 30). We are told that Jesus gave a loud cry at the hour of death, which is taken up by the letter to the Hebrews 'in the days of his flesh, Jesus offered up prayers and supplications, with loud cries and tears, to him who was able to save him from death, and he was heard' (Heb 5, 7), in the triumph of the resurrection.

Jesus teaches us to pray

2607 Prayer, according to Jesus' teachings in the Sermon on the Mount, depends on that state of heart in which we are reconciled with our brother, at peace with our enemies and persecutors and, going into our secret place have that purity of intention which is seeking the kingdom of God as its greatest treasure.

Mt 5,23–24
Mt 5,44f
Mt 6,14–15
Mt 6,6
Mt 5,8;
6,21.33

2610 We must then approach God with that *loving faith* that is able to say with Jesus, 'Abba! Father', through Him, with Him and in Him. There is nothing that we cannot be granted if we only believe without doubting: 'Therefore I tell you, whatever you ask in prayer, believe that you have received it and you will' (Mk 11, 24). This was the faith of the Canaanite woman (Mt 15, 28) and the centurion (Mt 8,10). It was because of the people's lack of faith that Jesus could not work miracles in Nazareth.

Mt 7,11f

Mk 9,23
Mt 21,22

Mk 6,5f

2612 Because the kingdom of God is near, prayer has *that urgency* that looks forward to Christ's second coming, no longer in weakness, but now in glory. S. Luke explains this in parable form; as with the insistent friend calling at night, so we must persevere; as with the persistent widow we must not grow weary; as with the tax collector we must have humility of heart, saying 'Lord, have mercy on me a sinner'.

Lk 21,34
Lk 11,5f

Lk 18,1f

2614 We must also ask in the name of him who at the right hand of God intercedes for us, and in union with him proclaim: 'Father, not my will be done, but yours'. The Holy Spirit is sent as another counsellor to intercede for us 'with sighs too deep

Jn 14,3

Lk 22,42

for words' (Rom 8, 26), so that we may ask in   Gal 4,6
Christ's name and be filled with gladness at being   Jn 16,24
heard.

Jesus hears our prayer

2616   The answer to prayer was given in the many cures
that Jesus worked during his life; in response to
those who asked in faith (the leper: Mk 1, 40–41;
Jairus: Mk 5, 36; the Canaanite on behalf of her
daughter: Mk 7, 29; the good thief: Lk 23:39–43);
or by those whose actions proved their faith (those
who let down the paralytic 'seeing their faith, he
said . . . 'My son, your sins are forgiven': Mk 2, 5;
the woman with a flow of blood: Mk 5, 28; the
sinful woman who anointed him with tears and
ointment: Lk 7, 37–38; those who cried out to
him 'Son of David . . . have pity on me': Mt 9, 27;
Mk 10, 48).

Chapter 3: The Prayer of Mary

2617   Mary represents that perfect acceptance of the will
of God, which is at the heart of all prayer: 'Behold
the handmaid of the Lord; let it be done in me
according to your word' (Lk 1, 38). In Cana she   LG 58
was moved with pity and begged her son to come
to the aid of the wedding banquet which was a sign
of that other wedding feast of the Lamb who gives
his Body and Blood at the request of the Church,
his Bride.   Rev 19, 7f

2619   The *Magnificat* (*Megalynei* in the Byzantine rite)
is the hymn of Mary Mother of the Church, the
new Eve and the daughter of Sion, and of all the
holy People of God who remember the mercy of
God 'as he spoke to our fathers, to Abraham, and
to his descendants for ever' (Lk 1, 54–55).

The Church also sanctifies the morning, noon and
evening with the *Angelus* which recalls the
annunciation by the angel and Mary's response,
concluding with the Incarnation of the Word of

God and the prayer that we may be brought by the Passion and Cross of her Son to the glory of His resurrection. It is an invitation during the day to pause for prayer. In paschal time it is replaced by the *Regina Coeli* in which the Church rejoices with Mary at the victory of the risen Christ.   MC 41

Chapter 4: The Church prays

2623   It was through the work of the Holy Spirit that the early Church persevered 'with one mind in prayer with the women, and Mary the mother of Jesus and his brethren' (Acts 1,14). He, who is sent to lead them into the fulness of truth, brings to mind   Jn 14,26 all that Jesus said, so that in their communion of prayer which was joined to the 'breaking of bread', they could express in formal rites and liturgical practice the heart of their faith.   Acts 2,42

Types of prayer

2626   *Blessing prayers* which recognize the gifts of God which bless us can be divided either into those which inspired by the Holy Spirit ascend through the action of Christ to the Father (Eph 1, 3—14; 2 Cor 1, 3—7; 1 Pt 1, 3—9), or those which ask for the grace of the Holy Spirit which comes from the Father through Christ (2 Cor 13, 13; Rom 15, 5—6,13; Eph 6, 23—24). *Prayers of adoration* arise from that humble awareness of the greatness of the Lord, the King of Glory who is 'Holy, Holy, Holy.' *The Prayer of petition* recognizes   Ps 24,9f that we depend on God as Creator, and as   95,1 Christians and sinners we look to him for   Rev 4,8 forgiveness: 'God, be merciful to me, a sinner' (Lk 18, 13). We begin every Eucharist by expressing sorrow for our sins, but our prayers of petition should seek first the kingdom of God : the   Mt 6,33 whole Body of Christ which so filled the heart of S. Paul that he wished to give himself totally for his brethren (Rom 10, 1; Eph 1, 16—23; Phil 1, 9—11; Col 1, 3—6.4, 3—4.12). Then our petitions should be directed to all our needs 'in everything by prayer and supplication with thanksgiving let

your requests be made known to God' (Phil 4,6).
Intercessory prayer, which 'does not consider the
things which are his own but those of others' (Phil
2,4), reminds the Christian that he is part of the
communion of saints, in which 'when one member
suffers all suffer together; if one member is
honoured all rejoice' (1 Cor 12,26). Such prayer
reaches out to all ... those in authority, and to   1 Tim 2,5-8
those who are our enemies and persecutors, as in
the dying words of Stephen, 'Lord, do not hold
this sin against them' (Acts 7,60). *Prayers of
thanksgiving*, which find their summit in the
Eucharist are so much a part of the Church's life
that S. Paul can say 'give thanks in all
circumstances' (I Thes 5,18). The *prayer of praise*
is that direct recognition of the glory of God, 'of
whom are all things, and we unto Him' (I Cor
8,6). The early Church took up the Psalms as their
praise of God in Christ, and in his vision, S. John
sees those who have come through the great
tribulation singing 'Alleluia! Salvation and glory
and power belong to our God' (Rev 19,1)   Rom 12,14

2630   The New Testament has scarcely any reference to
prayers of lamentation, due to the virtue of
Christian hope based on the resurrection; however
there is still that prayer that amounts to a sigh in
which we are part of the whole creation longing
for the fulness of redemption.   Rom 8,23f

The tradition of prayer

2650   Prayer cannot be reduced to a spontaneous
response to some inner instinct. The Church
grows in understanding of its faith and of its
prayer through contemplating the Scriptures and
allowing the heart to ponder on the spiritual
understanding which has been gained through
those who preach and teach the word of God.   DV 8

The sources of prayer

2653   The Church puts great emphasis on *the reading of
Scripture*, which should be part of our prayer   PV 47
because we talk to God when we pray and we listen   DV 25
to God when we read his words. Prayer is also that

essential response to the *Liturgy*, making it live in the heart of each person who is a member of the Church *believing, hoping and loving*. Yet there is also the promise which *each day* brings to sanctify the present moment by presenting it in prayer to God: 'O that today you heard his voice: harden not your hearts' (Ps 95, 7–8).

The way of prayer

2664   For the Christian there is only one way to pray to *God our Father* and that is by means of the sacred humanity of Jesus, prompted by the Spirit. We invoke *Christ* as Son of God, Word of God, Lord, Saviour, Lamb of God, King, Beloved Son, Son of the Virgin Mary, Good Shepherd, our Life, our Light, our Hope, our Resurrection, our Friend . . . But above all as Jesus (*YHWH saves*). In the East there is the version 'Jesus, Christ, Son of God, Lord, have mercy on us, sinners!'

2669   The Church praises the devotion to the Sacred Heart of Jesus and to his Holy Name, and encourages the Stations of the Cross, which allow us to follow our Saviour on that first Good Friday to his Cross and burial on Calvary.

2670   'Nobody can say "Jesus is Lord" but through the impulse of *the Holy Spirit*' (1 Cor 12, 3). The Holy Spirit leads us along the path of prayer and prompts our inspirations, so we should ask for his help, who is 'of all Consolers best', our Advocate: 'Come, Holy Spirit, fill the hearts of your faithful and kindle in them the fire of your love' (Sequence at Pentecost).

2671   The Byzantine *Troparion* (Hymn) at Pentecost is: 'Heavenly King, Consoler Spirit, Spirit of Truth who is everywhere present and fills all things, treasure of all goodness and source of life, come, dwell in us, purify us and save us, You who are good.'

In communion with Mary

2673   Mary, overshadowed by the Holy Spirit to become the Mother of God, is so totally associated with Christ that she is his *Sign*, his *Icon* who reflects the mysteries of His life. In the hymns and antiphons and prayers addressed to her we can note two aspects, one which glorifies the Lord for the great things he has done and the other which asks her to intercede for us. She is also that image of the Church praying, 'a sign of sure hope and comfort for the People of God'.

LG 68–69

2676   We can see this in the *Hail, Mary*. God himself rejoices over his chosen one whom he greets with the words of the angel, 'Hail, Mary ...'. She is declared 'full of grace' because 'the Lord is with thee', since she is the Ark of the Covenant, the dwelling place of God with men. Elizabeth will be the first of the many generations who will call her blessed among women (Lk 1,45), because by her faith she has become mother of all those who believe. We can pray to Mary because she has been given to us by her Son and is the Mother of Mercy to whom we commend every day that comes, especially the day of our death, that she may lead us to her Son in paradise. In the Middle Ages the *Rosary* evolved as a substitute for the Prayer of the Hours said by the priests and monks. It consists of fifteen decades which reflect of the mysteries of Christ and Our Lady. At the same time the *Salve Regina* or *Hail, Holy Queen* was composed. The East have developed the prayer of the Litany (Acathistós and Paráclisis), and Marian hymnology.

Lk 1,48
Zeph 3,17

Exponents of prayer

2684   The Holy Spirit raises up examples of holiness in every age who bear witness to the love of God in the devotion of their lives. They hand on to their disciples a share in their spirituality, which remains part of the rich treasury of prayer for the members of the Church, as does the whole of the Liturgy and Theology as it develops with the years.

Heb 12,1
2 K 2,9
Lk 1,17

2685 In addition there are also certain people who have a part to play in teaching us how to pray. In first place is the *family*, the 'domestic church', which teaches by the practice of daily family prayer. The *priests and deacons* form in prayer the people committed to them especially through the word of God which they preach. *Religious*, since the days of the monks of the Egyptian desert, give themselves to prayer and are sources of spirituality in consequence. *Catechetics* has as an aim that the truths of faith should become the subject of personal prayer. This will involve memorising basic prayers. *Prayer groups* which have sprung up in the Church are a sign of the desire to learn to pray. *Spiritual direction* is increasingly sought from those who have wisdom and discernment and are themselves experienced in the spiritual life.

PO 4

CT 55

Places for prayer

2691 The Church is above all the place for prayer, whether public or private, since one is able to adore Christ present in the Blessed Sacrament. But in the home there should also be a place where we can pray to Our Father in secret, or even an oratory. *Pilgrimages* also provide stimuli for prayer, since they are an image of our journey to God. *Retreats* allow us 'to go into the desert' to be alone with God.

Mt 6,6

PC 7

The life of prayer

2698 The Tradition of the Church provides us with a certain rhythm to help us to cultivate that habit of prayer. Day by day there is *Morning* and *Night Prayer, Grace before and after meals*, and the *Liturgy of the Hours*. Sunday is a special day of prayer and the liturgical year marks the passing of the seasons. There is supreme freedom to choose the way of prayer that the Lord guides us to follow. But there are three basic methods of prayer: *vocal, meditative and contemplative*.

Vocal prayer

2700 Vocal prayer is an essential part of Christian life.
When the disciples witnessed the silent prayer of
Jesus and asked him to teach them, he gave them
the *Our Father*. It is because we are body and soul   Lk 11,1
that we need to express the thoughts of our hearts
in common with Jesus when he blessed his
heavenly Father or turned to Him in his agony.
We cannot do without such external expressions,
but by realising who it is we are addressing, we
bring ourselves to the threshold of contemplation.

Meditation

2705 In meditation we try to channel our thoughts with
our imagination and desire to seek out what God
wishes of us. It is normal to use either a book (the
Scriptures or the works of a spiritual writer), a
liturgical text, a holy picture, or a favourite prayer.
Meditation allows us to deepen our faith and
strengthen our desire to follow Christ more closely.

Contemplation

2709 S. Teresa of Avila talked about prayer as 'being
alone with Him whom we know loves us'.   Life 8
Contemplation is that prayer of the one who gives
himself humbly to God, becoming aware of the
presence of God within us, which is a unique gift
allowing us to listen in silence, but which involves
those who give themselves to it in that struggle
which passes through the dark night to that light
which has no end.

The spiritual struggle in prayer

2725 As life itself is a struggle against our own
weaknesses and against the assaults of the devil, so
prayer mirrors that struggle: we pray as we live
because, we live as we pray.

Objections to prayer

2726 Some object to prayer because they do not
understand it correctly, they see prayer as a merely

psychological exercise, perhaps even to remedy an
interior emptiness. Others see it as an empty   Mt 6,7
mouthing of words. Others again regard prayer as
a wasteful intrusion into the busy pattern of their
day. These attitudes reveal certain *mentalities*
which prevent people from understanding the
nature of prayer, such as activism, utilitarianism
('what practical use can be ascribed to prayer'?)
rationalism (prayer cannot be analysed scien-
tifically and rationally), sensualism (whereas
paradoxically prayer is the love of true beauty
Philokalia) and escapism (true prayer in fact
enables one to live life to the full). Some also *give
up prayer* after they have started because they
experience dryness of spirit, or they become
disheartened because of 'the cares of the world
and the delight in riches' (Mt 13,22); or because
they do not seem to be heard; or again because of
the lack of humility which will not accept the
greatness of God and his mercy.

The need for humble vigilance of heart

2729   The difficulties encountered by those who enter
the struggle to pray include *distractions* which
come during the time of prayer. It is useless to
argue with them because this only exacerbates the
problem. Some writers claim that they are a
necessary stage in the journey to God and one
must gently bring the mind back to the subject.
Others say that distractions reveal the division in
one's heart which will only be resolved when one
'seeks the face of God' (Ps 27,8). There is also the
problem of dryness of spirit when there is no
enjoyment of thoughts and feelings in prayer.
This is a normal stage in the process, which
becomes the dark night of the soul in which one is
purified from one's attachment to the senses. It
can also be caused by one's shallowness. There is   Lk 8,6
also that hidden *lack of faith*, and of humility,
which either presumes on the love of God and
finds multiple reasons for not praying, or tends to
spiritual sloth (accidie), or even despair about
one's sinfulness, instead of that resolution that 'I
can do all things in him who strengthens me' (Phil
4,13).   Mt 26,42

Filial trust

2734 People cease praying because they think that their prayers are not heard. We need to ask why prayers are not answered and how prayer *is* in fact heard.

Unanswered prayer

2735 When we ask for things in prayer, do we think whether this request is in accordance with God's will? It is the Holy Spirit who helps us to pray as we ought and to intercede for what is in accord- ance with our need, for our Father knows our needs before we ask them. Otherwise we have divided loyalties and are unfaithful because in fact '(we) are asking wrongly, to spend it on (our) passions' (Jas 4,3). God wants to give us what is for our good.

Rom 8,26
cf. Mt 6,8

Effective prayer

2738 S. Paul is quite definite 'every one who calls upon the name of the Lord will be saved' (Rom 10,12). This is because Jesus' prayer is always heard by his Father and he prays for us and with us. If we unite our prayer to that of Jesus then 'everything (we) ask of the Father in my name will be granted (us)' (Jn 15,16).

Persevere in love

2742 There is a great need to persevere in prayer to counter our inertia and sloth and increase our love of God. The early Christians prayed *without ceasing* when Peter was imprisoned and we can do this if we unite prayer to action. Unless we pray, we will easily fall into sin and lose that love which unites us to the Father, with Christ who has so loved us, in the Holy Spirit.

Acts 12,5
Origen
Or 12
Mt 26,41
Rev 2,4

The prayer of the hour of Jesus

2746 Jesus prayed 'Father, the hour has come, glorify your Son, that your Son may glorify you'

(Jn 17,1). In that priestly action all time comes together, the love of the Lamb of God and the sin which betrayed him, the disciples gathered around and those who will believe in him; his passion and his resurrection. He delivers it all to his Father, having been given power over all flesh as Lord and High Priest interceding for us. He has also taught us how we should pray: 'Our Father ...'   Jn 17,2

Section II The Lord's Prayer : The Our Father

Our Father, who art in heaven,
hallowed be they name;
thy kingdom come;
thy will be done on earth as it is in heaven.
Give us this day our daily bread;
and forgive us our trespasses
as we forgive those who trespass against us;
and lead us not into temptation;
but deliver us from evil.

2759 In this way does Jesus respond to the disciples' request that he teach them to pray. There is a shorter version in S. Luke (11,2–4) but the Church has used the longer version of S. Matthew (6,9–13) in her liturgy. A doxology was soon added. The *Didaché* says 'The power and the glory are yours for ever'. The *Apostolic Constitutions* 8,2 adds 'Kingdom'. The Byzantine rite adds 'Glory be to the Father, Son and Holy Spirit'. The Roman Missal develops the last phrase, 'Libera nos a malo ...' 7,24,1

Chapter 1: A Summary of the Gospel

2761 All the Scripture finds its fulfilment in the Gospel of Christ which was announced in the Sermon on the Mount. Just as his life must be centred on his words, so our prayer must be centred on that prayer which he gives as the very heart of his Gospel, the *Our Father*, the most perfect of all prayers – indeed, the fundamental prayer. Aquinas ST 2–2,83, 9 Tertul Or 10

2765 We call it the *Lord's Prayer* not only because Jesus has given us this prayer himself (cf. Jn 17,7), but also because, being truly man, it is his prayer for the needs of all humanity. He also gives us the Spirit so that we may pray in confidence 'Abba! Father' (Gal 4,6).

2767 The Our Father is also the *prayer of the Church*. The early Christians recited the Lord's Prayer three times a day in place of the eighteen benedictions of the Jewish liturgy. In all liturgical traditions, the Our Father is an integral part of the *Liturgy of the Hours* and the Sacraments of Christian Initiation. In *baptism* 'those who are born again through the word of the living God' (1 Pt 1,23) learn to turn to God in prayer; in the Eucharist the Our Father which is placed between the Eucharistic Prayer and the Liturgy of Communion sums up all the previous petitions which have been made and prepares us to receive the Lord who is given as our daily Bread of Life, and look towards the coming of Christ in the glory of his kingdom.

Didaché 8,3

'Our Father who art in heaven'

2777 The Lord's prayer is introduced by a preamble in the liturgy 'We dare with confidence/ Make us worthy to ...' because we are coming into the presence of God who alone is holy, and we can only presume to do so because we have confidence 'to enter the sanctuary by the blood of Jesus' (Heb 10,19). It is he who says 'Here am I, and the children God has given me' (Heb 2,13).

Ex 3,5

2779 We say *Father* because he has revealed himself through his Son and his Holy Spirit, so that when we pray we are in union with him. We adore and bless him for having revealed his name and allowed us to believe in him, and for adopting us as his sons in baptism and making us other 'christs' by the anointing of his Holy Spirit. We have an obligation to behave as children of God, 'for that is what we are' (1 Jn 3,1) and it is to those who retain that childlike openness that the Father will continue to reveal himself.

Mt 11,25–2
1 Jn 1,3

GS 22
RC 4,9,1
Mt 11,25

2786 When we say *our* Father we are reminded like Israel of old that he is our God and we are his people. He is also our hope, for in the new heaven and new earth the one who conquers will hear it said 'I will be his God and he shall be my son' (Rev 21,7). In the Church all who are baptised share that new birth 'in the first born of many brethren' (Rom 8,29) in one communion with the same

Hos 2,21f.
6,1 – 6

Father in the one Spirit. We are also able to pray with those Christians who are separated from us that we may become truly one and that God, the Father of all, may draw together in love those who know him not.

UR 8,22
NA 5

2794   When we say *'who art in heaven'* we refer to the glory and majesty of God who is beyond all that we can imagine. It is also that home from which our sins have banished us and which has many rooms. It is because the Son of God has come down from heaven, and has ascended to his Father and ours, that we long 'for the shelter of that home which heaven will give us' (2 Cor 5,2) when we will be 'hidden with Christ in God' (Col 3,3).

Jn 14,2

Phil 3,20
Heb 13,14

The seven petitions

2804   The seven petitions are divided into the first three, which are directed towards the glory of the Father: his name, his kingdom, his will, that glory which has been given to him in his beloved Son, but awaits its fulfilment when creation is given back to him; and the last four which beg the Father of mercies for life and its final victory.

Jn 17,4

2807   We pray *'hallowed be thy name'* in the sense that we ask that God's name may be held holy. God reveals his name in the work of creation which shows forth his glory, and humanity wore the crown of that glory, but forfeited it by sin. He revealed his name to Moses and 'triumphed gloriously' over the Egyptians when the Israelites were brought out of slavery to become a consecrated nation and a holy people, who bore his name. But it is Jesus as Saviour (Mt 1,21;Lk 1,31) who makes known the Father's name which sanctifies in truth. In our baptism we were 'washed, sanctified, justified in the name of the Lord Jesus Christ and in the Spirit of our God' (1 Cor 6,11), and we are called according to the plan of God to be 'holy and spotless in his presence in love' (Eph 1,4). For our prayer is that his holiness may be made manifest in us, and through the sanctity of our lives and that the name of God may be blessed by all the nations of the earth.

Ps 8,6
Rom 3,23
Ex 19,5–6
Lev 19,2
Jn 17,7.17

'Thy kingdom come'

2816 The word 'basileia' can be translated kingship, reign, rule or kingdom, but it is already 'at hand' in Jesus, is announced by Him and is ushered in by his death and resurrection, until His final coming 'when he delivers the kingdom to God the Father' (1 Cor 15,24). We look towards that coming of Christ's kingdom which is of justice, love and peace. But that entails a struggle within us, so that we do not 'allow sin to reign in (our) mortal bodies' (Rom 6,12). We are also called to work in society for that true progress in which God's rights are respected, and like servants who have only done what was asked of them, we await the return of our Master: 'Come, Lord Jesus' (Rev 22,20).

> Cyril Cat Mys 5,13
> GS 22.32. 39.45.
> EN 31
> Lk 17,10
> Lk 12,36

'Thy will be done on earth as it is in heaven'

2822 The will of God is that extension of his kingdom on earth, 'a plan for the fulness of time, to unite all things in (Christ), things in heaven and things on earth' (Eph 1,9-10). In Christ that will is perfectly fulfilled, for he always did what was pleasing to his Father, even to giving himself up for our sins 'according to the will of our God and Father' (Gal 1,4). We must ask for the grace that our will may be united to the will of his beloved Son in that perfect obedience which sincerely seeks to know God's will and prays in communion with Christ, and Our Lady, as well as all those saints who have done the will of God.

> Heb 10,7
> Lk 22,42
> Rom 12,2
> Mt 7,21
> MR
> EP II 107

'Give us this day our daily bread'

2828 We turn to God who gives 'all things their food in due season' (Ps 104,27) and 'causes his sun to rise on bad and good alike' (Mt 5,45), confident in the providence of our loving Father, whose kingdom we seek and whose will we accept. However there is an added dimension caused by the starvation that exists in the world, and which invites us to have compassion on the poor and share our wealth with them, so that our abundance may supply their want. There is also that greater hunger for the

> Lk 6,1
> Dt 8,3
> Am 8,11

word of God, which we satisfy by the witness we bear to the Gospel and the whole missionary effort of the Church. This results in those who receive that word also receiving the Bread of Life, Christ our Eucharist, every day of their lives, and in their doing so with full confidence in our loving Father until *the day* they are admitted to the wedding banquet of the Lamb.

2834   Our food is a gift from God and therefore we should say *Grace before and after meals*, in acknowledgement of the Giver of all that is good.

'Forgive us our trespasses as we forgive those who trespass against us'

2839   With the confidence of the Prodigal Son, we admit our sinfulness to God, who stands ready to receive us because in His Son we have the remission of our sins, and in the sacraments the abiding sign of that redemption. Yet unless we are   Col 1,14
willing to pardon those who offend us, we will harden our hearts to the love of God and forget our constant need for His forgiveness, like the   Mt 18,23
debtor servant in the parable. Jesus explains to us   Mt 6,14f
that 'we must be merciful as our heavenly Father   Jn 13,34
is merciful' (Lk 6,36) we must love one another as he has loved us, forgiving one another 'as God in Christ forgave you' (Eph 4,32). This reaches even to our enemies, for such is God's compassion, as   Mt 5,43–4
the martyrs bear constant witness.   DM 14

'Lead us not into temptation'

2846   We ask God not to let us take the path that leads to sin, for God 'does not tempt anyone' (Jas 1,13). There is in fact that necessary testing which every Christian must submit to if he is to be worthy to follow Christ, but there is also that temptation which leads to sin and death, even though it might appear to be attractive and justifiable.

We will not be tempted beyond our strength, provided that we pray to God, mindful of the fact that Christ has overcome the devil who is the source of all lies and 'with the temptation provides the means of escape, so that (we) can successfully endure it' (1 Cor 10,13). We must however be on our guard at all times 'blessed is he that keeps watch and is clothed, so that he has no need to go naked, and be ashamed' (Rev 16,15).

'But deliver us from evil'

2850 Jesus does not pray that his disciples should be taken from the world, but that they should be kept 'from the evil one' (Jn 17,15). From the beginning Satan has set out to frustrate the plan of God, for Satan is 'a liar and the father of lies' (Jn 8,44). Yet even if he can be called 'the ruler of this world' (Jn 15,30) he has been conquered by Jesus 'who bore our sins in his body on the tree' (1 Pt 2,24) and who showed the power of his victory in the Immaculate Conception and Assumption of his Mother. We also pray that we may be delivered from all evil so that we can await in peace the glorious coming of our Saviour Jesus Christ, who is, who was and who is to come, to whom be glory for ever and ever.

1 Jn 5,18–19

Amen.

MR 126
Rev 1,8

Abbreviations

Books of Sacred Scripture quoted

Gen	Genesis	Jon	Jonah
Ex	Exodus	Mic	Micah
Lev	Leviticus	Zeph	Zephaniah
Num	Numbers	Zch	Zechariah
Dt	Deuteronomy	Mal	Malachi
Jos	Joshua	1 Mac	1 Maccabees
Jdg	Judges	2 Mac	2 Maccabees
Ruth	Ruth	Mt	Matthew
1 Sam	1 Samuel	Mk	Mark
2 Sam	2 Samuel	Lk	Luke
1 K	1 Kings	Jn	John
2 K	2 Kings	Acts	Acts of the Apostles
1 Chr	1 Chronicles	Rom	Romans
2 Chr	2 Chronicles	1 Cor	1 Corinthians
Ezra	Ezra	2 Cor	2 Corinthians
Neh	Nehemiah	Gal	Galatians
Tob	Tobit	Eph	Ephesians
Jud	Judith	Phil	Philippians
Esther	Esther	Col	Colossians
Job	Job	1 Thes	1 Thessalonians
Ps	Psalms	2 Thes	2 Thessalonians
Prov	Proverbs	1 Tim	1 Timothy
Eccl	Ecclesiastes	2 Tim	2 Timothy
Song	Song of Solomon	Tit	Titus
Wis	Wisdom	Heb	Hebrews
Sir	Sirach/Ecclesiasticus	Jas	James
Is	Isaiah	1 Pt	1 Peter
Jer	Jeremiah	2 Pt	2 Peter
Lam	Lamentation	1 Jn	1 John
Ez	Ezekiel	2 Jn	2 John
Dan	Daniel	3 Jn	3 John
Hos	Hosea	Jude	Jude
Joel	Joel	Rev	Revelation (Apocalypse)
Am	Amos		

Appendix I

The General Councils of the Church

A General or Ecumenical Council is an assembly of bishops normally called together to deal with a crisis in the Church. Canon Law states that such a Council must be convoked by the Roman Pontiff, presided over by him, either personally or through his delegates and transferred, suspended, dissolved and its decrees finally approved by him (CIC 338). There have been twenty-one General Councils.

1. First Council of Nicea, 325

It defined the divinity of the Word of God, against *Arianism*, using the term *homoousios*, consubstantial of the same substance (as the Father. Athanasius attended as a deacon.

2. First Council of Constantinople, 381

The theology of the Trinity was completed with the assertion of the divinity of the Holy Spirit against *Macedonianism* and the promulgation of the Creed which is essentially that used in the Mass.

3. Council of Ephesus, 431

The doctrine of the hypostatic union of the two natures in Christ and the declaration that Mary was *Theotokos*, Mother of God (against the heresy of Nestorius).

4. Council of Chalcedon, 451

The Fathers of the Council taught that there were two natures in Christ 'without their being any confusion or division or separation between them' against *Monophysitism*.

5. Second Council of Constantinople, 553

It confirmed the teaching of *Chalcedon* and condemned those who taught differently.

6. Third Council of Constantinople, 680–681

It taught that there were two activities and two wills in Christ, whereas the *Monothelites* maintained that there was only one will.

7. *Second Council of Nicea*, 787

The Fathers proclaimed the lawfulness of the veneration of icons and statues against the *iconoclasts* and the efficacy of the intercession of saints.

8. *Fourth Council of Constantinople*, 869–870

It recapitulated the teaching of former councils and moved to a normalization of relations between Constantinople and Rome.

9. *First Council of the Lateran*, 1123

It ratified the Concordat of Worms dealing with Investiture and renewed the strictures against simony and immorality.

10. *Second Council of the Lateran*, 1139

It issued thirty disciplinary canons, among which was one which mentioned the excellence of the law of continence for clergy and religious.

11. *Third Council of the Lateran*, 1179

It issued twenty-seven disciplinary canons relating to papal elections, the age for the reception of Holy Orders, benefices and the evil of usury.

12. *Fourth Council of the Lateran*, 1215

It taught that there is only one true God, the one creator of all things (against the *Albigenses*) that bread and wine are *transubstantiated* into the Body and Blood of Christ; that every Catholic is bound at least once a year to confess his sins and receive Holy Communion at paschal time. It issued seventy canons.

13. *First Council of Lyons*, 1245

It deposed the Emperor Frederick II and issued disciplinary canons connected with legal judgements. It again condemned usury.

14. *Second Council of Lyons*, 1274

The Council presided over by Blessed Gregory X with over five hundred bishops present declared that the Holy Spirit proceeds from the Father and the Son (*Filioque*); taught the validity of prayers for those in Purgatory, and laid down rules for the Conclave.

15. *Council of Vienne*, 1311–1312

It suppressed the Templars, gave principles to settle ecclesiastical disputes and declared that the rational soul is the *form* of the human body.

16. *Council of Constance*, 1414–1418

It ended the Western schism and elected Martin V. Only seven of its decrees, dealing with disciplinary matters, were confirmed.

17. *Council of Basel-Ferrara-Florence*, 1431–1445

An irenical Council which considered the differences between the Eastern Churches and Rome. It also decreed the matter and form of the sacraments, and gave a list of the books of the Bible.

18. *Fifth Council of the Lateran*, 1512–1517

A Council which legislated for reform and taught the immortality of the soul.

19. *Council of Trent*, 1545–1563

It was inaugurated on 13 December 1545 by Paul III, but transferred to Bologna in March 1547 before being suspended in 1549. This period produced decrees on Scripture and Tradition on Original Sin and Justification and on the sacraments in general and on baptism and confirmation. The second stage marked the reopening of the Council at Trent by Julius III from 1551–1552 and produced decrees on The Eucharist, Penance and Unction. The last period from January 1562 to December 1563 at Trent again produced the decrees on the Real Presence and the Sacrifice of the Mass, on Holy Orders, Matrimony, Purgatory, Images and Indulgences.

20. *First Council of the Vatican*, 1869–1870

It approved two dogmatic constitutions, *Dei Filius* on the nature of faith and the relationship of faith to reason and *Pastor Aeternus* on the universal primacy of the Roman Pontiff over the whole Church; and defined his infallible teaching authority.

21. *Second Council of the Vatican*, 1962–1965

This Council convoked by John XXIII made no dogmatic definitions but issued four Constitutions, nine Decrees and three Declarations. There were four sessions: October 1962–December 1962; September 1963–December 1963; September 1964–November 1964; September 1965–December 1965.

Appendix II

CATHOLIC PRAYERS

1. General Prayers

The Sign of the Cross

In the name of the Father, and of the Son, and of the Holy Spirit. Amen.

Our Father

Our Father, who art in heaven, hallowed be Thy name; Thy kingdom come; Thy will be done on earth as it is in heaven. Give us this day our daily bread; and forgive us our trespasses as we forgive those who trespass against us; and lead us not into temptation but deliver us from evil. Amen.

Glory be to the Father

Glory be to the Father, and to the son, and to the Holy Spirit. As it was in the beginning, is now, and ever shall be, world without end. Amen.

I Believe (The Apostles' Creed)

I believe in God, the Father almighty, creator of heaven and earth. I believe in Jesus Christ, his only Son, our Lord. He was conceived by the power of the Holy Spirit and born of the Virgin Mary. He suffered under Pontius Pilate, was crucified, died, and was buried. He descended to the dead. On the third day he rose again. He ascended into heaven, and is seated at the right hand of the Father. He will come again to judge the living and the dead. I believe in the Holy Spirit, the holy Catholic Church, the communion of saints, the forgiveness of sins, the resurrection of the body, and the life everlasting. Amen.

Prayer to the Holy Spirit

Come, Holy Spirit, fill the hearts of your faithful and kindle in them

178

the fire of your love. Send forth your Spirit and they shall be created. And you shall renew the face of the earth.

Let us Pray:

O God you have taught the hearts of the faithful by the light of the Holy Spirit; grant that by the gift of the same Spirit, we may be always truly wise and ever rejoice in his consolation. Through Christ Our Lord. Amen.

2. Morning Prayers

Morning Offerings

O Jesus, through the most pure heart of Mary, I offer you all my prayers, works, sufferings and joys of this day, for all the intentions of your Divine Heart in the Holy Mass.

Almighty Lord and God, protect us by your power throughout the course of the day, even as you have enabled us to begin it: do not let us turn aside to any sin but let our every thought, word and deed aim at doing what is pleasing in your sight. Through Christ our Lord. Amen

Almighty Lord and God, protect us by your power throughout the course of this day, even as you have enabled us to begin it : do not let us turn aside to any sin but let our every thought, word and deed aim at doing what is pleasing in your sight. Through Christ our Lord. Amen.

O angel of God, appointed by Divine mercy to be my guardian, enlighten and protect, direct and govern me this day. Amen.

3. Prayers during the day

An Act of Faith

My God, I believe in you and all that your Church teaches, because you have said it, and your word is true.

An Act of Hope

My God, I hope in you, for grace and for glory, because of your promises, your mercy and your power.

An Act of Charity

My God, because you are so good, I love you with all my heart, and for your sake, I love my neighbour as myself.

Acts of Contrition

O my God, because you are so good, I am very sorry that I have sinned against you and by the help of your grace I will not sin again.

O my God, I detest all the sins which I have committed against you. I am sorry that I have offended you because you are infinitely good, and sin displeases you. I love you with all my heart, and I firmly purpose with the help of your grace, to serve you more faithfully in the future.

I love you Jesus, my love above all things; I repent with my whole heart of having offended you. Never permit me to separate myself from you again. Grant that I may love you always; and then do with me what you will.

Prayer before work or study

Almighty God, be the beginning and end of all we do and say. Prompt our actions with your grace and complete them with your all powerful help. Through Christ Our Lord. Amen.

Prayers of Dedication

Teach us, good Lord, to serve you as you deserve; to give and not to count the cost; to fight and not to heed the wounds; to toil and not to seek for rest; to labour and to ask for no reward, save that of knowing that we do your will. Through Christ Our Lord. Amen.

(S. Ignatius of Loyola 1491 – 1556)

The things, good Lord, that I pray for, give me the grace to labour for.

(S. Thomas More 1478 – 1535)

Eternal God, who are the light of the minds that know you, the joy of the hearts that love you, and the strength of the wills that serve you, grant us so to know you that we may truly love you, and so to love you that we may truly serve you, whom to serve is perfect freedom.

(S. Augustine 354 – 430)

Holy God, Holy Strong One, Holy Immortal One, have mercy on us.
from *Good Friday Liturgy*

O God, come to my assistance: O Lord make haste to help me.
(Psalm 70,2)

Prayer for Vocations

O Lord Jesus Christ, who has chosen the Apostles and their successors, the bishops and priests of the Catholic Church, to preach the true faith throughout the whole world, we earnestly beseech you to choose from among us, priests and religious brothers and sisters, who will gladly spend their entire lives to make you better known and loved. Amen.

Prayer for the Pope

O God, eternal shepherd of your people, look with love on N. our Pope, your appointed successor to S. Peter on whom you built your Church. May he be the source and foundation of our communion in faith and love.
Through Christ Our Lord. Amen.
(Roman Missal, Votive Mass for the Pope)

The Stations of the Cross

The priest announces each Station and then says

V/. We adore you, O Christ and we bless you.
R/. Because by your holy cross you have redeemed the world.

After each Station all say an Act of Contrition

Our Father. Hail Mary. Glory be to the Father.
  1. Jesus is condemned to death
  2. Jesus receives his Cross
  3. Jesus falls the first time under the Cross
  4. Jesus is met by his blessed mother
  5. The Cross is laid upon Simon of Cyrene
  6. Veronica wipes the face of Jesus
  7. Jesus falls the second time
  8. The women of Jerusalem mourn for our Lord
  9. Jesus falls the third time
10. Jesus is stripped of his garments
11. Jesus is nailed to the Cross

12. Jesus dies on the Cross
13. Jesus is taken down from the Cross
14. Jesus is placed in the sepulchre

Prayer before a Crucifix

Behold, O good and most sweet Jesus, I kneel before you and with all the ardour of my soul, I pray and beseech you to engrave deep and vivid impressions of faith, hope, and charity upon my heart, with true repentance for my sins, and a very firm resolve to make amends. Meanwhile I ponder over your five wounds, dwelling upon them with deep compassion and grief, and recalling the words that the prophet David long ago put into your mouth, good Jesus, concerning yourself: 'They have pierced my hands and my feet; they have counted all my bones.'

XV Cent.

Prayer to S. Michael

Holy Michael, Archangel, defend us in the day of battle; be our safeguard against the wickedness and snares of the devil. May God rebuke him, we humbly pray; and do thou, Prince of the heavenly host, by the power of God thrust down to hell Satan and all the wicked spirits who wander through the world for the ruin of souls. Amen.

Grace before meals

Bless us, O Lord, and these your gifts which we are about to receive from your bounty. Through Christ Our Lord. Amen.

Grace after meals

We give you thanks, almighty God, for these and all your benefits who live and reign for ever and ever. Amen.

4. Evening Prayers

O my God, I adore you, and I love you with all my heart. I thank you for having created me and saved me by your grace, and for having preserved me during this day. I pray that you will take for yourself whatever good I may have done this day and that you will forgive me whatever evil I have done. Protect me this night, and may your grace be with me always and with those I love. Amen.

Visit, we beseech you, Lord, this dwelling, and drive far from it all the snares of the enemy; let your holy angels dwell herein, to preserve us in peace: and let your blessing be always upon us.

O my God, as I came from you, as I am made through you, as I live in you, so may I at last return to you and be with you for ever. Through Christ Our Lord. Amen.

O Lord, support us all the day long until the shadows lengthen and the evening comes and the busy world is hushed and the fever of life is over, and our work is done. Then, Lord, in your mercy, grant us a safe lodging, a holy rest, and peace at the last. Amen.

Cardinal Newman (1801 – 1890)

Save us Lord, while we are awake; protect us while we sleep; that we may keep watch with Christ and rest with him in peace.

from *the Office of Night Prayer*

5. Prayer before the Blessed Sacrament

My Lord and my God, I firmly believe that you are here; that you hear me and you see me. I adore you with profound reverence and I ask pardon for my sins.

Prayer after Holy Communion (The Anima Christi)

Soul of Christ, sanctify me.
Body of Christ, save me.
Blood of Christ, inebriate me.
Water from the side of Christ, wash me.
Passion of Christ, strengthen me.
O good Jesus, hear me.
Within your wounds, hide me.
Never permit me to be separated from you.
From the wicked enemy defend me.
In the hour of my death call me
And bid me come to you
That with your saints, I may praise you
For ever and ever. Amen.

Ascribed to Pope John XXII († 1334)

O Sacrament most holy, O Sacrament divine!
All praise and all thanksgiving be every moment thine!

My Lord and my God

(Jn 20,28)

6. Prayers to Our Lady

Hail Mary

Hail Mary, full of grace, the Lord is with thee; blessed art thou among women, and blessed is the fruit of thy womb Jesus. Holy Mary, Mother of God, pray for us sinners, now, and at the hour of our death. Amen.

Hail Holy Queen

Hail Holy Queen, mother of mercy; hail our life, our sweetness, and our hope! To thee do we cry, poor banished children of Eve; to thee do we send up our sighs, mourning and weeping in this vale of tears. Turn then, most gracious advocate, thine eyes of mercy towards us; and after this our exile, show unto us the blessed fruit of thy womb, Jesus. O clement, O loving, O sweet Virgin Mary.
Pray for us, O holy Mother of God
That we may be made worthy of the promises of Christ.

The Memorare

Remember, O most loving Virgin Mary, that it is a thing unheard of, that anyone ever had recourse to your protection, implored you help, or sought your intercession, and was left forsaken. Filled therefore with confidence in your goodness I fly to you, O Mother, Virgin of virgins. To you I come, before you I stand, a sorrowful sinner. Despise not my poor words, O Mother of the Word of God, but graciously hear and grant my prayer.

Prayer for Our Lady's Protection

We fly to thy patronage, O holy Mother of God; despise not our petitions in our necessities, but deliver us always from all dangers, O glorious and blessed Virgin.

III Cent.

The Rosary

The Joyful Mysteries
'Behold I bring you news of great joy'. (Luke 2,10)

1. The Annunciation Our Father ... Ten Hail Marys. Glory be ...
2. The Visitation
3. The Birth of Our Lord
4. The Presentation of Jesus in the Temple
5. The Finding of Jesus in the Temple

The Sorrowful Mysteries
'He has surely borne our griefs and carried out sorrows' (Isaiah 53,4)

1. The Agony of Jesus in the Garden
2. The Scourging at the Pillar
3. The Crowning with thorns
4. Jesus carries His Cross
5. The Crucifixion

The Glorious Mysteries
'God has highly exalted Him and bestowed on Him the name which is above every name.' (Philippians 2,9)

1. The Resurrection
2. The Ascension
3. The Descent of the Holy Spirit on Our Lady and the apostles
4. The Assumption
5. The Coronation of Our Lady in heaven.

Hail, Holy Queen ... (see beginning of section)

Let us pray:

O God, whose only begotten son, by His life, death and resurrection has purchased for us the rewards of eternal life; grant, we beseech thee, that meditating upon these mysteries in the most holy rosary of the Blessed Virgin Mary, we may both imitate what they contain and obtain what they promise. Through Christ Our Lord. Amen.

The Angelus

The angel of the Lord declared unto Mary
R/ And she conceived by the Holy Spirit. Hail Mary ...
Behold the handmaid of the Lord
R/ Be it done to me according to your word.

Hail Mary ...

The Word was made flesh
R/ And dwelt among us. Hail Mary ...
Pray for us, O holy Mother of God
R/ That we may be made worthy of the promises of Christ

Let us pray:

Pour forth, we beseech you, O Lord, your grace into our hearts, that we to whom the Incarnation of Christ your Son was made known by the message of an angel, may, by his Passion and Cross, be brought to the glory of his Resurrection. Through Christ Our Lord. Amen.

Regina Caeli
(recited in place of the Angelus during Eastertide)

Queen of heaven, rejoice! Alleluia.
For he whom you merited to bear, Alleluia.
Has risen, as he said. Alleluia.
Pray for us to God. Alleluia.

V. Rejoice and be glad, O Virgin Mary, Alleluia.
R/ For the Lord has risen indeed. Alleluia.

Let us pray:

O God, who through the resurrection of your Son,
Our Lord Jesus Christ, willed to fill the world with joy,
grant, we beseech you, that through his Virgin Mother,
Mary, we may come to the joys of everlasting life.
Through the same Christ Our Lord. Amen.

7. Prayers for the Faithful Departed

The De Profundis (Psalm 130)

Out of the depths, I have cried to you, O Lord.
Lord hear my voice.
Let your ears be attentive.
To the voice of my supplication.
If you, O Lord, shall observe iniquities,
Lord, who shall endure it?
For with you there is merciful forgiveness;
And by reason of your law, I have waited for you,
O Lord.
My soul has relied on his word;
My soul has hoped in the Lord
From the morning watch even until night
Let Israel hope in the Lord.
Because with the Lord there is mercy
And with him plentiful redemption.
And He shall redeem Israel
from all his iniquities.

Prayers for deceased relatives and friends

Almighty Father, source of forgiveness and salvation, grant that our relatives and friends who have passed from this life, may, through the intercession of the Blessed Virgin Mary and of all the saints, come to share your eternal happiness. Through Christ Our Lord. Amen.

Prayer for all the Holy Souls

O God, the creator and redeemer of all the faithful, grant to the souls of your servants departed the remission of all their sins, that through our pious supplication they may obtain that pardon which they have always desired; who live and reign for ever and ever. Amen.

Prayer for the Dying

In the name of God the almighty Father who created you,
in the name of Jesus Christ, Son of the living God who suffered for
    you,
in the name of the Holy Spirit, who was poured out upon you,
go forth, faithful Christian. May you live in peace this day,
may your home be with God in Zion, with Mary the virgin Mother of
    God,
with Joseph, and with all the angels and saints.

Commendation

Jesus, Mary and Joseph, I give you heart and my soul
Jesus, Mary and Joseph, assist me in my last agony.
Jesus, Mary and Joseph, may I breathe forth my soul in
peace with you.

Eternal Rest grant to them, O Lord
And let perpetual light shine upon them. May they rest
in peace. Amen.

May the souls of the faithful departed, through the
mercy of God rest in peace. Amen.

May the Lord bless us, may he keep us from all evil and bring us to
life everlasting. Amen.

LIST OF ABBREVIATIONS

AAS Acta Apostolicae Sedis
A G Ad Gentes
Ambrose
  de *myst*eriis
  de *viduis*
  de *virg*initate
Anselm
  *pros*logion
Aquinas
  collationes in *decem praec*eptis
  Summa *C*ontra *G*entiles
  Summa *T*heologiae
Athanasius
  *epi*stula *festi*valis
Augustine
  de *civi*tate *Dei*
  *con*fessiones
  contra *Faust*um manichoeum
  *enchiri*dion de
    fide, spe et caritate
  con*tra* epistolam Manichoci
  quam vocant *fund*amenti
  quaestiones in *Hept*ateuchum
  Homiliae
  de *libero*arbitrio
  de *mend*acio
  ennaratio in *Psalmos*
Bonaventure
  in libros *sent*entiarum
CA Centesimus annus
CD Christus Dominus
CDF Congregation for the Doctrine of the
  Faith
*Chrys*ostom
  in *Lazarum*
CIC Codex Iuris Canonici (Code of Canon
  Law)
CL Christifideles Laici
Const Council of Constantinople
CT Catechesi tradendae
Cyril (of Jerusalem)
  *cat*echeses illuminandorum
  *cat*echeses *myst*agogicae
DC Dominicae cenae
DH Dignitatis humanae
DM Dives in misericordia
DS Denzinger-Schönmetzer
DV Dei verbum
Egeria
  *pereg*rinatio ad loca sancta
EN Evangelii nuntiandi
EP Eucharistic Prayer
*Faust*us of Riez
  de *Spiri*tu Sancto
FC Familiaris consortio
Flo Council of Florence

GCD General Catechetical Directory
GS Gaudium et Spes
Hermas
  *Visi*ones pastoris
HG Humani Generis
HV Humanae Vitae
Ignatius of Antioch
  epistula ad *Rom*anos
IM Inter mirifica
Irenaeus
  *A*dversus *H*aereses
Jerome
  *comm*entariorum in *Is*aiam
John Damascene
  de *F*ide *O*rthodoxa
John of the Cross
  Ascent of Mount *Carm*el
J B Jura et bona
Justin
  *apol*ogiae
Lat Lateran Council
Leo I
  *Serm*ones
LE Laborem exercens
LG Lumen Gentium
MC Marialis cultus
MD Mulieris dignitatem
ME Mysterium Ecclesiae
MF Mysterium Fidei
MR Missale Romanum
NA Nostra aetate
Newman
  *Apol*ogia
  *Diffi*culties of Anglicans
  Sermons on *Subj*ects of the *Day*
Nic Council of Nicea
Nic-Con Niceno-Constantinopolitan
OE Orientalium ecclesiarum
OP Ordo poenitentiae
Origen
  de *or*atione
OT Optatam totius
PC Perfectae caritatis
PH Persona humna
Pius XI
  *Casti Con*ubii
  *Q*uadragesimo *A*nno
Pius XII
  *Hauri*etas *aquas*
  *My*stici *Corp*oris
  *H*umani *G*eneris
PO Presbyterorum ordinis
Polycarp
  *marty*rium Polycarpi
PP Populorum progressio
PV Pastores Dabo Vobis

RC Roman Catechism
RM Redemptoris Missio
Roman Catechism
RP Reconciliatio et poenitentia
SC Sacrosanctum concilium
SPF Solemn Profession of Faith (Paul VI)
SRS Sollicitudo rei socialis

Tertullian
 de *oratione*
Tol XI Council of Toledo
Trent Council of Trent
UR Unitatis redintegratio
VS Veritatis splendor

INDEX

*An asterisk indicates an entry under appendix 1 or 2